MW00332243

About Island Press

Since 1984, the nonprofit organization Island Press has been stimulating, shaping, and communicating ideas that are essential for solving environmental problems worldwide. With more than 1,000 titles in print and some 30 new releases each year, we are the nation's leading publisher on environmental issues. We identify innovative thinkers and emerging trends in the environmental field. We work with world-renowned experts and authors to develop cross-disciplinary solutions to environmental challenges.

Island Press designs and executes educational campaigns, in conjunction with our authors, to communicate their critical messages in print, in person, and online using the latest technologies, innovative programs, and the media. Our goal is to reach targeted audiences—scientists, policy makers, environmental advocates, urban planners, the media, and concerned citizens—with information that can be used to create the framework for long-term ecological health and human well-being.

Island Press gratefully acknowledges major support from The Bobolink Foundation, Caldera Foundation, The Curtis and Edith Munson Foundation, The Forrest C. and Frances H. Lattner Foundation, The JPB Foundation, The Kresge Foundation, The Summit Charitable Foundation, Inc., and many other generous organizations and individuals.

The opinions expressed in this book are those of the author(s) and do not necessarily reflect the views of our supporters.

Sundressed

Sundressed

NATURAL FABRICS AND
THE FUTURE OF CLOTHING

Lucianne Tonti

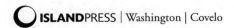 **ISLAND**PRESS | Washington | Covelo

Library of Congress Control Number: 2022941569

All Island Press books are printed on environmentally responsible materials.

Manufactured in the United States of America
10 9 8 7 6 5 4 3 2 1

Keywords: carbon footprint, circular economy, clothes recycling, fast fashion, hemp, microfiber, modal, natural fabrics, organic cotton, organic farming, polyester, regenerative agriculture, secondhand clothing, silk, sustainable fashion, synthetic fabrics

For my Dad

Contents

Introduction

I love my clothes. It's what I say anytime someone tells me they don't want to be seen in the same thing twice. I love my clothes. On a good day, they make me feel beautiful. On a bad day, at the very least, they help me feel composed.

I love the way a pair of pants can feel empowering. I love the way a mid-length skirt with a slit feels when I walk. I love the flash of leg from a certain angle on the street or sitting in a chair. I love the way a well-tailored suit provides balance across the shoulders, through the waist, hips, and sleeves. I love styling: the right coat with the right dress. Something sexy with something boyish. Something pretty with something tough. I love the softness of silk layered with the softness of cashmere. The crispness of a good cotton shirt against a pair of jeans. I love throwing an oversized coat over athletic gear, a cocktail dress, pajamas. I love the theatre of dressing, the play of it. The way an outfit can make a night feel exciting. The way an outfit adds color to memories, to the energy of a moment, to how it felt on that street corner, in that restaurant, at that hotel bar.

I'm not interested in clothes I can only wear once. I want clothes to carry me through the seasons of a year, of my life. I want clothes that see me through job interviews, the end of relationships that never even began, dinner parties with new friends, birthdays with old friends, weddings, funerals, dancing. Our clothes are some of our most intimate companions: how do you get to know them if you only wear them once?

How do you know that a particular jacket will get too hot if the sun comes out? Or that the rub of that waistline will be uncomfortable through a long dinner? How do you know that a dress will make you feel so wonderful you don't have to think about it, aside from when you're receiving compliments? How do you know that putting things in certain pockets will upset the line of the hip, so you do need to carry a bag? Or in that knit dress, you can get away with not taking a jacket. And in that skirt, you can walk fast, but you can't run. That those shoes hurt when you're dancing. That those pants will crease if you sit down for too long. That you can rescue your white blouse from red wine because it's been spilled on before. That while you can zip yourself into the bodysuit, you need a friend to help take it off. How do you know which dresses, shirts, and pants are comfortable enough, beautiful enough, and resilient enough to see you through an entire day, from meetings to dinner?

A world where you don't know your clothes sounds awfully risky. It sounds like a recipe for days with itchy necklines, clammy armpits, and having to carry your too-warm jacket. And of course, it's risky for the planet too, although risky is an understatement. A world where we don't know our clothes, where we wear them a handful of times before we throw them away, is more than risky. It's disastrous.

Fashion's carbon footprint and environmental offenses have been thoroughly documented by academics, reported on by the biggest management consulting companies in the world, and investigated by very talented journalists. The latest reports suggest fashion is responsible for two percent of global greenhouse gas emissions, although some estimates place it as high as ten percent, not to mention the pollution of waterways, the harm to workers along its supply chains, and the insurmountable levels of textile waste generated every second by clothes we have thrown away or donated to charity. The clothes we never got to know. The clothes we didn't fall in love with.

For several years now, the fashion industry has been on a mission to become more sustainable – or at least to convince people that it is. The use of the word *sustainable* and its counterparts – *conscious, eco, natural, positive impact, zero waste* – have become so ubiquitous, so overused in PR and marketing campaigns, that they have come to lose their meaning. Or in fact, their meaning is so deliberately vague that the truth about a garment's impact is successfully obscured.

That's not to say there aren't innovations. Sustainable "solutions" are arriving hard and fast: biological and technical inventions; recycling; renewable technologies; closed-loop production systems that recycle water and chemicals; waste management and circularity; increased transparency to allow for greater traceability, visibility, and accountability. The pace is exciting, but that list is exhausting not least because scratching the surface of most of these solutions can prove extremely unsatisfying. Transparency is no good without standardized language and proper accountability. Closed-loop production can refer to just one part of the production process. Circularity and recycling technology are in their infancy: without large-scale infrastructure to capture, sort, and process textile waste, most garments will not be recycled – and by most, I mean ninety-nine perent, no matter what the PR copy claims.

Aside from this, it is impossible for the fashion industry to reduce its carbon emissions while rates of consumption and production continue to climb, and despite the posturing and the summits, the voluntary codes of conduct and the coalitions, neither show any signs of slowing down. At least not while current systems and thinking remain in place. It's not just the industry that needs to change. Our understanding of clothes needs to change too. We have lost sight of the origins of these garments and materials that have kept us warm and made us feel beautiful for centuries. We have lost sight of the people who make them, who have the knowledge and skill to pleat, stitch, and tailor. Production was outsourced decades ago, prices dropped, marketing infiltrated our lives, and the amount of clothes we bought increased – some estimates suggest by double.

That's all without considering that polyester, a plastic made from fossil fuels, represented 52 percent of the global fiber market in 2020.[1] And it has somehow received such great publicity that writers of life cycle assessments are convinced it is one of the most sustainable materials, because they classify it a by-product of fossil fuels. The logic of this is so skewed it's hard to believe, especially since we have been denouncing plastic for clogging up oceans and strangling fish for the last decade. Polyester sheds microfibers of plastic pollution into waterways every time it's washed – microfibers that end up in the bellies of sea creatures and in our soils – and the implementation of technology to prevent this is extremely slow. Right now, anything labeled recycled polyester is actually just downcycled plastic, so degraded that its next stop is landfill.

And besides, polyester is uncomfortable. It has a complicated relationship with oil, by which I mean it attracts it, absorbs it, and won't let it go. It also has a complicated relationship with sweat and body odor, for much the same reason – that is to say, polyester smells and that smell is impossible to wash away. We shouldn't be wearing it. It doesn't belong against our skin. But my clothes that are made of natural fibers – cotton, linen, silk or wool – I would take them with me to the ends of the earth.

In April 2018, I was in Milan for a week for work. At the time, I was living in Paris and working for an Italian designer, and our small team had piled onto the train to set up an exhibition and pop-up shop at the Salone del Mobile, a design fair. It was a particularly warm spring. The sky was a faultless blue – perfect weather for the designer's clothes. Each morning, I pulled on one of her shirtdresses or kaftans and slid my feet into leather sandals. Over the course of the day, I felt the light fabric wick moisture from my skin as I ran between our temporary store and various exhibitions or aperitifs on the sprawling terraces Milan is famous for. The dresses had deep pockets and long, wide sleeves that could be rolled up or down, depending on the breeze. They were both utilitarian and sophisticated, which meant they could be worn from breakfast to dinner. They were soft and airy, and so comfortable I felt present, in my body, and relaxed, like I was on holiday.

The Italian designer was also a stylist. She worked out of a light-filled atelier in the ninth arrondissement of Paris, and I worked there with her for two years. Together with her partner (a photographer) and her talented protégé, she created clothes made exclusively of natural fibers. She had an intense obsession with *savoir faire* – and the ability to contextualize the wearer of her clothes within a landscape. The consideration of sun and wind, heat and movement, meant she created clothes that felt alive against the body. They were made in limited runs, a tactic designed to instill in her customers the value of scarcity, to unlearn years of conditioning that encouraged everyone to consume more, to wait for sales, to follow trends.

It is to our detriment that mass production and the abundant supply of cheap clothing has desensitized us to the connection between our clothes and their origins, between our clothes and the land. Take the example of the dresses I was wearing in Milan; they were made of cotton. When you see cotton growing in a field, it is completely mesmerizing. It is a fluffy white ball that grows like a flower on a bush, and can be plucked from the plant, bright white, clean, and practically ready to be spun into yarn and woven into a garment. The reason the dresses in Milan were so comfortable is because on the body, cotton reacts to temperature. It breathes when you are hot and provides warmth when you are cold. It is durable and supple. This flexibility makes sense when you consider that the particles in a cotton shirt once belonged to a plant photosynthesizing energy from the sun. Another natural fiber, wool, is similarly alive. Its complex molecular structure makes it resistant to wrinkles, stains, and water. It is elastic, soft on the skin, and breathable. It is warm, comfortable, and protective. Linen is lightweight and gets softer and smoother with each wear; the flax plant from which it is derived turns fields across France and Belgium pale blue for just a few weeks every year. Silk is drawn from a cocoon; it shimmers like water, but a single filament is stronger than steel.

These fabrics are some of nature's most incredible creations. But in our highly convenient world, where we have optimized our lives for next-day delivery to benefit from global trade and created a hierarchy that ranks working at a desk above working on the land, we've completely lost sight of the fact that our clothes come from the soil. They are the product of the natural world, and we're lucky to get to wear them. Unfortunately, like most parts of fashion's production, farming natural fibers on an industrial scale can be harmful to the environment. But there is another way. These fibers, these precious materials that can make you fall in love with your clothes, can be farmed in ways that heal and regenerate the earth.

This type of fiber farming is often referred to as *regenerative agriculture*. Broadly speaking, regenerative agriculture is derived from Indigenous land management practices and can be thought of as a kind of "beyond organic" farming. Like organic, it shirks the use of synthetic pesticides and fertilizers, but then goes further, aiming to improve ecosystems, soil health, and water cycles. A variety of techniques can be implemented, such as multi-species planting and integration of livestock, and the soil is never tilled. The farm is not simply a group of paddocks with an output of crops; it is part of the natural world and managed using principles of holistic stewardship, so the health of the landscape is always actively improving. Some of the obvious metrics include the return of native trees, grasses, insects, and animals, and an increase in the organic matter of the soil so that it is soft, fluffy, and dark brown, like chocolate cake. This indicates the soil has a healthy biological life, with micro-organisms exchanging nutrients including nitrogen and carbon through photosynthesis and building mycorrhizal fungi – which are important for substantial crop yields. Another metric is improved water cycles so that the soil retains more moisture, meaning the farm is less vulnerable to droughts. Extensive research shows that restoring soil health through this type of agriculture is an efficient way of pulling carbon out of the atmosphere and returning it to the ground. This is exciting because, of the earth's natural carbon sinks – plants, sea, soil, and sky, soil is one of the safest places to store carbon.

For the imperiled fashion industry, regenerative agriculture presents an intriguing solution. By using it to farm cotton, flax (linen), silk, wool, cashmere, and hemp, the industry could theoretically move beyond merely mitigating harm to supporting healthy landscapes in regions the industry has typically used and abused. Farmers who have switched to these techniques say they are happier and more relaxed, that they have a sense their land is coming back to life. What's more, some of the biggest players in the fashion industry are early adopters. Patagonia and Kering (whose brand empire includes Gucci, Bottega Veneta, and Saint Laurent) are already training cotton farmers across their supply chains in the principles of regenerative farming.

Of course, the issues within the fashion industry are too complex to be solved by simply changing the way its raw materials are farmed. There also needs to be a return to localized production; more investment in renewable energies to run the factories that convert raw materials from fleece to yarn to textile; and significant analysis of the chemicals used along the supply chain to dye, smooth, and make our clothes shine. But starting with the source, with a sheep's fleece or a cotton boll, can enhance our connection to and appreciation of our clothes. This is important if we are to subvert the cycle of buy-and-dispose and trans-form our relationship with them – while still getting to wear beautiful things. Importantly, it means we can wear clothes that have improved the health of landscapes, and the lives of the animals and people that live on them.

In the following pages, we'll look at both the way fibers are farmed and the way they are transformed into garments. We'll visit rangelands in Mongolia where cashmere goats are herded from highlands to desert, American fields where collectives of farmers are growing cotton beneath the heat of the Californian sun, and small villages in China where mothers and daughters weave buttons by hand. We'll uncover the layers of ingenuity and resources embedded in each t-shirt, coat, or dress. Through this exploration, we can reorient our understanding of each garment we buy, each garment we wear, around the valuable resources it contains, and wonder at the ability of a flower on a plant to become a shirt, or the fluffy fleece on a sheep to be cleaned and spun into a turtleneck. Hopefully this shift in understanding will mean we take better care of our clothes and enjoy wearing them for longer so we can reduce our appetite for newness.

It's a seductive proposition, one with the potential to resolve the tensions between our desire to wear beautiful clothes and our desire to have a truly sustainable fashion industry. It's a vision for a hopeful future, one that promises rewilding of fields, pastures, rangelands, and meadows while offering farmers and communities more sustainable livelihoods – a future in which we understand the value of our clothes and get to know them, so that we can confidently say, I love my clothes.

CHAPTER 1
There Is No Such Thing as Sustainable Fashion

I have a black dress that swings through the skirt down to the mid-calf. It has a slight slit on one side that shows a little leg while you're walking and a little more at a run. It is sleeveless. The waist is slightly dropped and sits just above my hips. It is cut on the bias. I can wear a jacket over it when there is a nip in the air. It is the perfect length for my long coats. I wear it with brogues and boots, with sandals and heels. I love to wear it on dates. It is effortless in the best sense, by which I mean it is both comfortable and flattering. I could name several important events in my life that I have worn it to. Job interviews. Dinners with new friends in new cities, when I was anxious and unsure of leaving the house. I could tell you about nights I abandoned it on a beach in a town I didn't live in so I could run into the water, knowing I could shake the sand out later. I have worn it backstage at Burberry runway shows in London. I have worn it on press trips to Tokyo, Dubai, Marrakech and Milan. It has recovered from splashed olive oil, anxiously sponged out in restaurant bathrooms. It has pockets. It is made of viscose so before it was a dress, it was a tree.

Most of our clothes are products of nature. Linen trousers begin as a flax plant largely sustained by rainwater. Silk is a protein secreted by the silkworm and spun into its surrounding cocoon as a continuous double filament thread. The cotton in your shirt grows like a flower turning sunlight into sugar to feed the soil.

Most of our clothes are products of nature and when we're talking about sustainable fashion, we should hold this knowledge close. Especially now, when the term is so overused in PR and marketing campaigns, its meaning has become profoundly confused. Long before brands began to send out emails promoting recycled materials and organic cotton, or promising net-zero emission denim and positive-impact shirts, Professor Sandy Black described sustainable fashion as an oxymoron in *The Sustainable Fashion Handbook,* which was published way back in 2012. The term has not gained greater clarity in the decade since.

Between 2018 and 2020, the amount of clothing described as sustainable on websites from the United States and the United Kingdom more than doubled.[1] This reflects growing consumer awareness of the threat of climate change: in a recent McKinsey & Company poll, more than three in five consumers cited sustainable materials as an important factor in their purchasing decisions. But unfortunately, the description alone doesn't mean much: in the fashion industry the term *sustainable* can be applied by anyone to almost anything.

Can fashion ever be sustainable? This is a question often posed to me at dinner parties. For a long time, I thought the answer was no – that true sustainability meant wearing and repairing what you already owned, buying new clothes and vintage pieces sparingly. I advised the designers I worked with that the best way to minimize the impact of their collections was to make only pieces of the highest quality from natural fibers, that could be loved, cherished, and worn for at least ten years. These conversations about design were often centered on how beauty and desire are essential to sustainability, because it's the clothes we love – the black dress that makes us feel confident, the coat that makes us feel composed – that we take the best care of, that we keep forever.

If buying clothes for a ten-year time frame sounds expensive, that's because it is. But it doesn't mean you need to spend more money on clothes; it's about apportioning the money you already spend differently. Take for example, a pair of pants: instead of buying four or five pairs of pants a year, you take the total amount you would normally spend on all those pairs and buy one beautiful pair. This can be described as a prerogative only available to the middle class and above, which is a fair criticism. But price and quality are the simplest ways to make people buy less and value what they already own more. And while fast fashion may seem like a democratization of style, the communities being harmed further down the supply chain shouldn't be forgotten. Most garment workers are women who exist on the margins and don't get paid a living wage. Purchasing clothes with a higher price doesn't guarantee that the people who made your clothes are being paid fairly, but generally, the price tag reflects what it cost to make the garment, a percentage of which should have been paid to the makers.

When we're talking about price and inequity in fashion from the perspective of a consumer, it's worth remembering that before fast fashion, clothes were made to last. They were worn, re-worn, and repaired. Now, clothes are often so poorly made they fall apart, stain easily, and start to smell, so they have to be constantly replaced. This means that anyone who buys fast fashion because it is all they can afford ends up worse off. A better solution to the expense of sustainable fashion is to learn what good quality craftsmanship and fabrics feel like and buy secondhand. Long term, the hope is that as sustainable fashion becomes more widespread, economies of scale will make it more affordable. But unfortunately, the path to an accessible sustainable-fashion system is a long and winding (sometimes treacherous) road.

To begin with, among all the promises and posturing, there are two essential things to understand about sustainable fashion. The first is that the sheer volume of clothes being made, bought, and thrown away is at the heart of fashion's carbon footprint. The second is that it's extremely difficult to ascertain what sustainable fashion actually is: the experts argue about everything from the direction of big structural changes to the merits of recycled polyester, organic cotton, and vegan leather.

That first point is just about the only thing sustainable fashion advocates and industry leading researchers do agree on: there will be no significant mitigation of the industry's carbon footprint while rates of production and consumption continue to rise. Recent projections suggest global clothing consumption will rise by sixty-three percent between now and 2030, the equivalent of approximately five hundred billion t-shirts.[2] These projections wipe out any of the industry's progress toward sustainability or carbon neutrality, with the 2019 Pulse of the Fashion Industry report declaring that "fashion companies are not implementing sustainable solutions fast enough to counterbalance the negative environmental and social impacts of the rapidly growing fashion industry."[3]

Rates of production and consumption began to climb when the free trade agreements of the late 1990s and early 2000s slashed protections for the clothing and footwear industries, meaning businesses could move production to less-developed countries where labor and materials were cheaper and there were fewer environmental regulations. A 2016 study by McKinsey & Company revealed that the average person buys sixty percent more clothing than they did before these changes occurred and keeps each item for about half as long.[4]

Take, for example, this statistic: the average American woman owns seven pairs of jeans.[5] The cotton in those jeans was likely grown using an unimaginable amount of water, which may have been irrigated from waterways needed by local communities. Estimates of the exact amount vary widely, with the UN putting the number at 7,500 liters per pair, while Levi's says it's roughly 2,565. The cotton was also likely sprayed with pesticides that destroy soil health and biodiversity. It then could have been picked by Uyghur slaves in China and was likely spun into yarn and woven into fabric in mills that release carbon into the atmosphere because they are powered by coal. Finally, it may have been dyed with toxic chemicals that were released into waterways, poisoning workers and those living nearby. This might all seem hyperbolic or simply the price we pay in a capitalist society for comfort and convenience, but to make matters worse, those jeans are likely to be thrown away after a few years.

When you are trying to determine the ecological impact of a specific garment, the fashion system is complicated and convoluted. There are several steps along the production line of the jeans I just described that could have been more sustainable – like using organic cotton which, according to a 2014 report, produces forty-six percent less CO_2 than the conventional variety.[6] But if the cotton was shipped from India to China, where it was processed in factories with poor environmental and humanitarian standards only to be manufactured into jeans that were worn a mere seven times before being discarded, the good generated by them being made from organic cotton is pretty futile.[7] To make matters worse, in 2022 the journalist Alden Wicker revealed that much of the "certified" organic cotton on the market may not be organic at all, thanks to an opaque and corrupt certification system.[8]

The wider system operates in a more linear way that is easier to understand: take, pollute, discard. Huge quantities of resources or raw materials are extracted from the earth to produce clothes. This production requires lots of electricity and chemicals that burn even more fossil fuels, and at the end of a garment's life, if it doesn't biodegrade, like plastic, it will sit in landfill. According to a 2017 report, one garbage truck of textiles is landfilled or burned every second.[9] The textile industry uses ninety-eight million tons of non-renewable resources per year to produce synthetic fibers, fertilizers to grow cotton, and chemicals to make, dye, and finish fibers and textiles.[10] McKinsey & Company estimates that seventy percent of fashion's greenhouse gas emissions come from raw material production, preparation, and processing.[11]

One of the reasons we find it so difficult to grasp the environmental cost of fashion is because we outsourced production decades ago. Now, Western countries produce very little: in 1990, half of all clothing worn in the United States was made here, but local manufacturing currently accounts for just two percent of all clothing sold in America. In Australia, it's six percent, and most clothing sold in the United Kingdom is made elsewhere.[12] This offshoring means we don't see fields ravaged by pesticides or plumes of thick gray smoke being chugged into the air by factories. We have no idea that the magenta hue of our favorite dress will cause the river in our town to run a deep shade of pink because of the wastewater from the dyeing process.

Maybe we were never really conscious that the cotton in our t-shirts was grown in a field, that the sheep roaming the hills produce the soft fleece in our knitwear. Certainly, the rise of polyester further distanced us from the idea that the natural world had been the source of our clothes for centuries. This should be cause for alarm because polyester is a plastic derived from fossil fuels, and the greenhouse gases emitted while extracting it and processing it into a fiber are very hard to quantify. Scientists estimate that half a million tons of plastic microfibers are released from synthetic clothing like polyester and nylon into our oceans, mountains, rivers, and soil every year, which is equivalent to more than fifty billion plastic bottles.[13] Horrifyingly, polyester is now ubiquitous, largely because it has always been cheap and easy to produce at scale. It has caused a race to the bottom on price and quality, as natural fibers have been forced to compete with synthetic counterparts that were billed as fibers of the future. Alongside this, consumer attitudes shifted and, in a few short decades, value systems that once placed quality over quantity, natural over artificial, and local production over cheap prices disappeared.

The first time I wore the black dress was to a party in a run-down mansion on the beach in Melbourne. It was a party that happened every summer. The weekend before Christmas, the boys who lived in the house would put on Hawaiian shirts and string fairy lights across the backyard. Over the course of the evening, guests would disappear across the sand and come back with damp bottoms and dripping hair. After sunset, the DJ would relocate upstairs and we would keep dancing, the party spilling out onto a balcony overlooked by an enormous palm tree, the straight line of the water stretching out behind it. I'd bought the dress secondhand that afternoon and hadn't thought twice about its fabric composition or carbon footprint. Sitting on the balcony, beneath the branches of this grand old palm, waiting for the sun to appear over the horizon, it didn't occur to me that the viscose dress I was wearing had also begun as a tree sprouting from the earth.

The debate around viscose illustrates a fundamental problem within the fashion industry and is a good example of how the word *sustainable* can be misleading. The viscose in my dress would have been made from a fast-growing tree like pine or eucalypt. Two hundred million of these trees are logged every year to make viscose, which is a type of rayon (*rayon* being the umbrella term for manufactured cellulose fibers that largely come from trees, including modal and lyocell). Viscose sourcing has been linked to the destruction of endangered and ancient forests.[14] This is devastating, as trees help guard against the warming of the planet because they pull carbon out of the atmosphere. Scientists estimate better management of tropical forests, mangroves, and peatlands could provide twenty-three percent of the climate mitigation needed to meet the objectives outlined in the Paris Agreement.[15]

To add insult to serious injury, more than half of each tree is wasted during the next stage of production – the process of turning the tree into fiber or yarn. This involves dissolving wood pulp in a chemical solution to create a thick substance, which is then extracted into strands that are spun into fibers and woven into fabric. The chemicals used in viscose production are highly toxic, and exposure has been linked to higher levels of disease in the people who work in the factories and those who live nearby, including coronary heart disease and blindness, as well as psychological and neurobehavioral disorders.[16] The process also results in the toxic pollution of air and waterways. Manufacturing rayon is so toxic that in 2013, the United States Environmental Protection Agency banned its production. Even so, global use of rayon doubled between 2005 and 2015.[17]

Despite this, the fashion industry and many sustainable fashion advocates consider cellulose fibers like viscose and rayon to be eco-friendly because they are derived from renewable sources (trees), they are less toxic than polyester and, unlike polyester, they can biodegrade and re-enter the biocycle. Canopy, a non-profit that works to ensure large-scale forest conservation, has done its best to prevent trees from being sourced from ancient and endangered forests, and to ensure manufacturing is carried out using a closed-loop system that protects workers and the environment, but the systems are far from perfect. Sustainable fashion pioneer and designer Stella McCartney sources all the viscose in her supply chain from forests in Sweden that are managed in a way that mimics nature's patterns of disturbance and regeneration, protecting their productivity and biodiversity for generations to come. But as author and environmentalist Rebecca Burgess writes in her book *Fibershed*, "The primary issue remains – using tree pulp for clothing is a land- and fossil-fuel-intensive process that puts our precious global forests at risk."[18]

Given how complicated these issues are, it should come as no surprise that there is no real consensus about what constitutes best practice. Because fashion supply chains are so convoluted, it can be really tough to understand what has happened at each stage of production. This is why a lot of brands claiming to be eco-friendly will shout about transparent supply chains and traceability, and though both assist with account-ability, without agreed-upon industry standards and specific language, visibility into a supply chain doesn't guarantee anything. The industry is also awash with certifications that cover everything from organic farm-ing to carbon neutrality, but because these programs are voluntary, they often lack independent oversight and the resulting certifications can be tantamount to greenwashing. This lack of clarity extends to statistics that are commonly thrown around in conversations between experts and in news reports about the industry, like "The fashion industry is the second largest polluter in the world." It's more accurate to say that fashion is responsible for between two and ten percent of global green-house gas emissions. Taking into account variances across years and in credible reports, it places somewhere between the fourth or tenth most polluting industry.

In addition to all these challenges – the convoluted supply chains, resource use, pollution, and untenable rates of production and con-sumption – it's worth considering the end goal. Given that we are already witnessing the severe impacts of one degree of warming—the wildfires, flash floods, heatwaves, droughts, and biodiversity loss—what exactly we are trying to sustain? The world has no use for sustainable fashion, we need something more. We have to go beyond processes that merely mitigate the harm caused by reducing emissions and switch to techniques that heal landscapes and regenerate the earth.

One of the first collections I watched the Italian stylist create in Paris was inspired by Anafi, a tiny, wild island a thirteen-hour ferry ride from Athens. The four of us traveled there together, late in the summer, to shoot the campaign. The rooms of our hotel opened onto expanses of sea and sky. The island was just remote enough to deter the crowds, creating a meaningful sense of escape from the real world. It had rolling hills so high and steep that, driving down them, you felt you might topple into the ocean.

Before we left, the designer gifted me a twinset from that collection. It was made of a beautiful mustard cotton that had delicate light- and navy-blue pinstripes running vertically through the fabric. The pants were wide-legged and high-waisted with double front-facing pleats and deep side pockets; the matching shirt was oversized, with long sleeves and a mandarin collar. The fabric had a specific weight; it was thick and stiff and lightly coated so it had a soft sheen. It was heavy enough to wear on a warm night without a jacket and light enough for the heat of the high summer sun. The first time I wore it was to dinner on the island. We sat on the balcony of a family-run tavern that looked straight out to the Aegean Sea. We drank local wine and ate octopus, a yellow split pea dish called *fava*, and *horta* – a plate of wild greens. As we walked back to the hotel after dinner, the designer commented, "We are wearing Anafi, in Anafi."

I have worn that outfit so much and so often; in the first year I owned it, I must have worn it once a week. I've worn it to drinks at the Ritz in Paris and to the beach in Palermo. I've worn it under big knits and heavy coats in London. It was what I wore when I caught the train to Munich to meet my brother and his girlfriend, who had moved there from Oslo. I wore it to greet my other brother and his boyfriend when they arrived at the Grand Hotel Amour in Paris. I have worn it so much that once, at a dinner in Milan, an old friend of the stylist remarked he'd never seen me in anything else.

In a 2011 interview with British newspaper *The Independent*, the American designer Marc Jacobs declared, "What survives the whole process is what people wear ... I'm interested in clothes people want, covet, desire, wear, use, love, tear, soil. Clothes mean nothing until someone lives in them."[19] Clothes make up the details of our lives, and understanding why we love some clothes and wear them more than others is key to reversing the patterns of consumption and disposal that are at the heart of fashion's carbon footprint.

A 2018 study revealed that we don't wear at least fifty percent of our wardrobes.[20] According to the Ellen MacArthur Foundation, in the United States, clothes are worn for a quarter of the global average, and in China, clothing utilization has decreased by seventy percent in fifteen years.[21] The founder of Fashion Revolution, Orsola de Castro, writes in her book *Loved Clothes Last,* "The average British woman hoards approximately 285 pounds worth of unused clothing."[22] One of the most meaningful things we can do to make fashion more sustainable is to keep our clothes for longer and to wear them more often, thereby reducing the need for replacement consumption.

The year before I moved to London, I worked for an Australian designer with fastidious attention to detail. He lived in a house built into the side of a sun-drenched hill that overlooked Tamarama beach with his girlfriend, who was the fashion editor of Australian *Vogue.* His clothes were made in Australia from beautiful fabrics he imported from Europe. His stores were made of concrete and glass, and from every corner you could see an element of nature. The flagship store on Oxford Street in Sydney stretched long and dark toward a counter that sat beneath a roof that opened via a mechanism onto the sky.

I wore a coat from my last season with him for years. It was a thick boiled wool with wide leather sleeves and a dropped shoulder. The collar was broad and, because the lapels dived deep into a double breast with a single line of buttons, the collar could be popped, and the coat wrapped around the body against the weather. It had pockets inside and out, a single pleat that ran down between my shoulder blades, and a solid, low-hanging half-belt that was fixed to the back. It was lined with a heavy satin viscose. It was long, it fell well below my knees, and hung across my shoulders with such weight that whenever I was in it, I felt *ready.*

I wore it to a dinner party when I first arrived in Paris over black jeans and a turtleneck. The host asked me to leave my shoes at the door and, without the coat and the heel of my brogues, the outfit felt flat. Halfway through the aperitif, the door opened to a guest the sight of whom made me curse my lack of footwear even more. It was the best, oldest friend of someone I had fallen out with in London and was very much hoping to forget. We smiled and small-talked our way through dinner, while I desperately hoped she wouldn't recount tales of my bad behavior to my new Parisian friends. We happened to leave the party at the same time, and when she and her girlfriend said goodbye to me under the yellow streetlamps, I felt suddenly self-conscious of my aloneness and embarrassed of my vulnerability, trying to build something in this new city. But when I turned my back on them, I felt the coat move around me. I knew the two inches the brogues added to my height made the coat swing and as I walked away and heard the clip of my heels on the cobblestones, I felt sure that everything was going to be all right.

What the coat gave me in that moment was some emotional resilience and a kind of protection. Not like the physical protection we get from clothes – warmth or shelter – but protection, nonetheless. It was the type of protection the late fashion photographer Bill Cunningham described when he said, "Fashion is the armor to survive the reality of everyday life." If all we needed from our clothes was insulation or reinforcement, we could simply and efficiently meet those needs. But what we get from clothing is so much more – belonging, self-expression, comfort – and the volume of resources we consume to satiate these is incredible. Professor and author Kate Fletcher describes how, "In the context of fashion, the resource intensity of our need for identity formation, communication, and creativity as expressed through our dressed bodies is also the chief challenge for durability."[23] We now buy more clothes than we ever have before, and we wear them less – sometimes we don't even wear them at all before we discard them. Fletcher goes on to say, "No industry has better perfected the cycle of invention-acceptance-dissatisfaction-invention than fashion; and has so successfully de-linked it from physical need or function." I think this is because we are always searching for a garment that makes us feel stronger, calmer, more beautiful. Fashion has captured our imagination by making us believe it can change something fundamental about our lives, about ourselves. I'm inclined to believe the right outfit can.

Sure, this has some insidious implications: fashion plays on our insecurities and acts as a signal for status and wealth in a world where income inequality means the super-rich have perverse amounts of political influence. It operates using a deeply sexist paradigm that profits off women as both consumers and workers; it reinforces unhealthy body image, whiteness, ableism, and has a troubling obsession with youth. But dismissing it as frivolous and superficial, acting like it's not something worth serious analysis, distracts from our ability to understand it. Like it or not, we all participate in the industry every day, every time we put on clothes. As Miuccia Prada said in a *New Yorker* interview in 1994, "Everybody makes a choice when he or she gets dressed ... It's not true when people say, 'I don't care what I have on.' Your way of dressing is something you can go to the psychoanalyst to find out about, because there are so many personal things involved."[24] If we could understand why some items of clothing inspire us to feel a certain way, we would be closer to understanding how to make all our clothes endure. We would be closer to subverting the cycle of invention-acceptance-dissatisfaction-invention.

Another time I wore the coat was to a job interview at a café in Pimlico on a cold but sunny Sunday morning. I was meeting a creative consultant for Burberry who needed an office manager and PA; I was running out of money fast and needed a job. The interview posed a challenge to dress for: the consultant worked in high fashion, split her time between

London and New York and, from her Instagram, I could see she was friends with models like Anja Rubik and movie stars like Sienna Miller. I wanted to impress her, and it felt like a meeting to which I should wear high heels and a good dress, but it was a Sunday morning and I didn't want to look desperate. I settled on a soft black sleeveless shirt, tucked into high-waisted tailored pants with a cigarette leg and trainers. The coat made the outfit; I knew it elevated the pants and shirt – *it was a piece* – and this knowledge helped ease my nerves.

Working for this woman gave me an insight into a totally different part of the fashion industry: luxury. The size and scale of the operations at Burberry dwarfed any designers I've worked with before or since. Luxury brands are behemoths, churning out such a volume of product that the word *luxury* has lost its meaning. What used to be signified by artisanal craft, workmanship, and expertise has been substituted by mass-produced premium products. According to Orsola de Castro, "We started to believe in the shine and not the substance, in designer logos over human hand-print."[25] In the last decade, the luxury goods industry has been totally transformed by realizing huge growth, aided significantly by expansion into Asia. Before COVID-19 hit, the value of the personal luxury goods market was €281 billion.[26] This reflects the sheer volume of product sold, most of which has come to be mass-produced in much the same way as fast fashion – a side effect of which is over-production. In 2018, the BBC reported that in a five-year period, Burberry had destroyed unsold clothes and perfume to the value of £90 billion.[27] The rationale offered by the company was that they didn't want the stock devalued by selling it at a discount or on the 'gray market'.

This gets to the heart of one of fashion's biggest issues, and an issue with manufacturing more broadly. The more units produced in a single production run, the cheaper the price per unit. This is because fabric can be bought in bulk, lowering the price per yard, and cutting fabric can be done en masse, saving the factories time. The result is a system that incentivizes brands to order more so they can sell each garment at a better margin. Meanwhile, capitalism has seen companies relentlessly pursue growth for decades.

The industry has created systems to sustain these endless cycles of more, like the never-ending global fashion market, which moves between the four fashion capitals: New York, Milan, London, Paris. These markets and their runways, showrooms, and parties occur four times a year, each spanning an entire month. In the last ten years, they have been propelled into front-row view by the rise of social media, influencer culture, and our insatiable fascination with celebrities. Of course, COVID-19 brought all of this to a grinding halt and gave the entire industry the opportunity to finally pause and reflect on what we had been doing, rather than trying to discuss it through our jetlag over warm prosecco and the too-loud music of yet another magazine launch in the Marais.

But the truth is, the damage has already been done. The endless treadmill we had been running on, always looking to the next collection, one line-sheet and look-book away from burnout, fed the system we call fast fashion (which Orsola de Castro thinks is not so distinguishable from fast luxury), and it has fundamentally changed our psychological relationship with clothes. The boom of social media and camera phones meant images of runway shows (once exclusive events that were never photographed) could be beamed around the world for immediate consumption, and fast fashion companies such as Zara and H&M perfected the art of knocking off next season's designs and getting them onto the shop floor in a matter of weeks. The temporal nature of each trend and their perpetually moving goalposts instilled the idea that newness is integral to fashion, creating a consumer mindset that could only be satisfied by the gratification of another purchase. Various reports describe how members of Gen Z refuse to re-wear an outfit once they've posted a photo of themselves in it on social media – the terrifying amalgamation of free market and toxic psychological forces. Kate Fletcher describes this as psychological obsolescence: "In order for the prevailing business model's bottom line to keep showing growth, garments have to become obsolete, at least in psychological terms."[28] Of course, with declining quality, fabrics, and craftsmanship, they often become obsolete physically too.

In my very early twenties, I found a pair of men's Comme des Garçons suit pants at a thrift store. I had them slightly tailored and wore them everywhere and to everything for almost ten years. They had a single pleat at the front and sat just above my hips; the wool was firm but soft and withstood being treated terribly on grimy dancefloors and in university pubs. I was late for a meeting the first time I tore them. I slipped on the pavement when I was running to get the train and they ripped across my right knee. I was so upset I couldn't listen to a single thing my editor had to say. Instead, the refrain "I tore my pants" bounced around my head while the graze on my knee stung. I got a tailor to do a crude repair and went on wearing them. The second time they tore was years later, in Paris. I was writing in my kitchen. I tucked my knees up under my chin, leaned my shins against my dining table, and heard them split along the bottom. This time, I was too broke and unsure of my French to take them to a tailor, so I begged a skilled friend to repair them for me. When he gave them back, he warned, "That fabric is so old, beautiful but old, you're literally wearing it out." A few weeks later, they tore again, and I didn't have the heart to let them go. Right now, they are trapped in storage with my coat in my friend's basement: there are oceans between us and I think about them at least once a week.

Had these pants meant less to me, I might not have repaired them. Had they been less comfortable or stopped working with the rest of my wardrobe, I might not have repaired them. Had they been made with less skill, had the fabric been cheaper, had the zip broke, I might not have repaired them. But they were made to last, and I was determined to make them last. It was Joan Crawford who advised we "care for our clothes, like the good friends they are." Durability and sustainability go hand in hand: every time we lengthen a product's lifespan by repairing it so that we refrain from buying something new, we are curbing our carbon footprint. Fletcher believes we also benefit psychologically from behaviors that extend the life of our garments, that taking steps to care for and mend objects that are important to us "may contribute to feelings of well-being as they help satisfy inherent psychological needs for competence, relatedness and autonomy."[29]

Of course, getting our clothes repaired is a labor of love, driven by the value we place on each item. It helps if the item is one of substance, designed with durability and utility in mind, with craftsmanship that makes repairs possible. I believe it helps if we spent enough on the piece to bring its monetary value front and center in our minds, so that we are invested in its longevity. The low cost of fast fashion is constantly given as a rationale for the thoughtless disposal of clothing, and it has conditioned us to believe that these intricate garments, made by someone sitting behind a sewing machine, made from precious resources and someone's creativity, cost nothing to create. Fashion should be expensive, or at least, more expensive than it currently is. But really, I point to price as a way to capture something greater, to capture why we might care enough about an item of clothing so that we bother to get it repaired, to continue wearing it. To desire something enough that, time and time again, we reach for it in our wardrobes – fashion is, after all, a game of hearts and minds.

Above everything else, the mustard twinset was both comfortable (which is why I wore it so often) and durable (which meant I could wear it frequently without fear of damaging it). It was made of a very special woven cotton. As I've mentioned, cotton has unique properties on the body, one of which is its ability to provide insulation and protect the wearer against the heat or the cold. This is because the fabric traps air between its fibers, creating a layer of protection. Cotton is also strengthened by water, meaning it can be washed repeatedly. The wool in my overcoat had been boiled so the fibers had shrunk and wrapped around each other tightly, which meant the air had been removed; the result was a thick, felt-like fabric. It didn't let heat out or the cold in; its density and width repelled water but it also had a lightness that made it a pleasure to wear. The compressed and interlocked fibers meant the coat was resistant to friction, so even after years of wear, it was still beautiful. Designing clothes with materials that last is one of the most practical ways to extend the life of a garment; the benefits of selecting fabrics to enhance durability and desirability are enormous. Material choice is also one of the simplest ways to lessen a garment's environmental impact and, by highlighting this, we can bring the origins of our clothes back into focus. Fashion is inextricably bound to nature, and this shouldn't be lost on us as we try to navigate the complex questions of how to lessen the industry's carbon footprint.

Appreciating the beauty of the natural world offers hope for the fashion industry in two different ways. The first is about enjoyment. Clothes made of natural fibers are more comfortable against our skin and more beautiful in form and drape, which should mean we enjoy wearing them and value them more than synthetic fibers. We become more attached to our clothing when we remember the precious resources from which they are made—the goat or the paddock or the ecosystem that produced them. The second is if we change the way we farm fibers, they can drive positive outcomes for nature, from the sheep on the hillside to the native birds in the fields where cotton is grown, from the wildlife across degraded rangelands to the waterways in the mountains in China where hemp is farmed. In all these places, on all these farms along fashion's convoluted supply chains, we can regenerate landscapes, waterways, soil health, and biodynamic ecosystems. The combination of these two forces — a love of clothes and a love of nature — could subvert the take-make-waste model that is driving fashion's enormous environmental footprint.

CHAPTER 2

Fashion that Doesn't Cost the Earth

On the second-to-last day of 2020, I met a farmer. He was bearded and broad-shouldered and described himself as "no nonsense" before he poured me a glass of wine. He told me that in 2016, he bought his father's share of the family farm for a dollar. His story was one I would come across again and again in my reading, a kind of fable with lessons and warnings.

When his uncle and father bought the property, they implemented what they believed were best practices in order to achieve the highest crop yields possible. These techniques included cutting down trees, spraying chemicals like fertilizers and pesticides, and tilling the soil – the hallmarks of industrial agriculture.

In the years that followed, the farm's profitability plummeted. All farms endure extreme weather events that can affect profitability – droughts, floods, or wildfires that can be written off as bad luck, an inescapable part of an unpredictable line of work. But farmers with keen eyes say that despite being at the whim of weather patterns, they know something else is happening to their land. The bearded farmer told me he knew the farm was in trouble when he tried to break the ground with a shovel and couldn't. The soil was depleted; the plants were less productive; insect varieties had vanished; birds were scarce. At the same time, the costs of the chemicals and machinery were high, backing the farm into a toxic cycle of debt.

If this sounds like a nightmare, that's because it is. Imagine following the advice of experts and investing huge amounts of money under their direction, only to watch your crops and soil become depleted as the landscape around you grows increasingly inhospitable. It would rightly drive you crazy before it broke your heart.

This pattern has been repeated again and again across continents, from Africa to Asia, from America to Europe. Everything from the soybeans in our tofu to the cotton in our jeans is farmed industrially, using principles that increase yields in the short term but, we now understand, destroy the land in the long term.

The environmental consequences of industrial agriculture are well documented: the destruction of biodiversity, the acidification of oceans and, worst of all, the depletion of soils and the release of carbon stores into the atmosphere. In 2014, a senior United Nations official declared that if we continue to farm using the principles of industrial agriculture, we only have about sixty years of topsoil left. While this figure has been questioned, there is widespread agreement that the amount of arable land per person is declining significantly and quickly.[1] In an article for *The Griffith Review*, Australian farmer and author Charles Massy issued the following warning: "It is clear we have entered a new, dangerous era for life on earth. Human activity has begun to overwhelm the great forces of nature, placing virtually all life – including that of humanity – at potential grave risk."[2]

On a local scale, farmers are left with exhausted lands and no money to keep investing in the chemicals on which they have come to depend. Some understandably give up, but others seek out alternatives. The bearded farmer worked with some of the best chefs in the world and, through exposure to beautiful produce and the forward-thinking farmers who grew it, he developed a different understanding of best practice from his father's generation. He embraced regenerative agriculture and began to prioritize soil health and biodiversity.

The farmer describes his new approach as "best practice for the land that we have." He stopped using pesticides and synthetic fertilizers and started intercropping – planting different species between the main crop to build nutrients in the soil. Initially, the farmer's yields were lower, but because he had no large bills to pay, his profit margin improved and in just five years, the land had come back to life. His experience has been mirrored by grain and fiber farmers, ranchers, ecologists, naturalists, and scientists from across the globe.

It is a story that is full of hope, and not hope based on futile recommendations to be more diligent about recycling plastic, to change light bulbs, or take shorter showers. It is big, full-hearted hope, the kind that makes your chest expand when you're walking through a forest and the morning sunlight comes in low through the trees – the kind of hope you feel when you dive deep under salty waves, beneath the yellow of the summer sun and look out across the blue to the horizon. This hope is tangible. It's not driven by industry or invention. It relies on knowledge so ancient it hurts to think what we have destroyed and overlooked in our quest for more units, faster production cycles, and cheaper t-shirts.

A lot of this knowledge is drawn from Indigenous and Native land stewards, from techniques that have been used for longer than most of us can comprehend – techniques based in understanding that the health of the landscape is inextricably linked to the health of people who manage it, techniques that focus on care for and renewal of the natural world. It is grounded in reverence for plants and wildlife, for mountains and rivers, for sunshine and rain. In her book *Braiding Sweetgrass: Indigenous Wisdom, Scientific Knowledge and the Teachings of Plants,* Robin Wall Kimmerer explains, "Our lands were where our responsibility to the world was enacted, sacred ground. It belonged to itself; it was a gift, not a commodity, so it could never be bought or sold."[3]

Before the development of industrial agriculture, before the scientific revolution, worship of the natural world was widespread. For millennia, the dominant belief system of many human societies was animistic and centred on the magic and mystery of nature. The earth was viewed as sacred, and humanity had a moral obligation to protect it. The wind, thunder, and shadows were thought to possess a living soul. Plants, animals, rocks, rivers, and mountains had feelings. Animism is associated with the concept of the organic mind, or organicism, under which humans are deeply entwined with their environment. In these belief systems, which remain at the heart of many Indigenous cultures, humans' relationship with nature is spiritual, ritualized, and non-hierarchical. Each is connected with the other. Over centuries, the prominence of these belief systems evolved and changed. A gradual shift occurred, particularly in the West, and society's ability to be enchanted by the natural world was diminished. This shift from the organic to the mechanical mind precipitated the free-market ideologies that dominate the global economy today and gave rise to the technologies on which industrial agriculture depends.

In 1840, a German named Justus von Liebig became the first scientist to rationalize the use of synthetic fertilizers. He believed harvesting crops removed nutrients from the soil, so he created something called the balance-sheet theory – the idea that farmers should return the nutrients they took from the soil by fertilizing it with a combination of nitrogen, phosphorous, and potassium. It's a concept advocates of industrial agriculture still believe in today.

The technological advancements of both world wars accelerated the development of agricultural chemicals. In the early 1900s, a German

Jewish chemist, Fritz Haber, made chemical breakthroughs that transformed the German war effort, and the dominate-and-destroy mantra of industrial agriculture became deeply entwined with some of the world's darkest history. He synthesized chemicals for use in explosives and poisonous gases, including ammonium, which would eventually be used to make Zyklon B, the lethal gas of Hitler's concentration camps. In 1918, he won a Nobel Peace Prize for the Haber-Bosch process of "fixing" nitrogen, which transformed modern agriculture via the fertilizer ammonium nitrate.

When ammonium nitrate fertilizer is applied to a crop, it usurps the natural cycle by adding nutrients to the soil. Synthetic fertilizers allowed farms to be run like factories, transforming inputs of raw materials into outputs of crops. The logic of biology was replaced by the logic of industry, and food and fiber could be produced at economies of scale. Because chemicals temporarily increase yields, global cotton production has tripled, even though the total area of land dedicated to cotton growing has not changed in ninety years.[4] We now understand that the widespread application of synthetic fertilizers damages the soil by disrupting the connection between soil microbes and plant roots. It also results in the release of the harmful greenhouse gas nitrous oxide, leads to the contamination of waterways, and harms ecosystems by oversaturating them with nutrients.

This pattern of short-term gain and long-term losses creates a cycle of problems that requires more money, machinery and chemicals to fix. The productivity of the land becomes dependent on continual meddling from the outside. For instance, intensive tillage (plowing) and monocropping (planting only one type of crop) deplete the nutrients in the soil; to compensate for this, farmers apply synthetic fertilizers. All three of these techniques reduce the soil's ability to store moisture, which means the land needs more irrigation. Monocropping also leads to infestations of weeds and insects, requiring the use of pesticides. Plants have to withstand these chemical inputs and so seeds are genetically modified to do so … and the list goes on. Charles Massy says industrial agriculture techniques "tend to be implemented and integrated without regard for their unintended, long-term consequences … The frequent result has been an intermeshing of counterproductive practices that are destroying ecological systems."[5] The long-term implications of this system are alarming – to say the least – and it's now clear a holistic view to landscape management is essential. But for a long time, industrial agriculture was seen as a way to feed the world and facilitate population and economic growth.

Textile manufacturing was one of the first industries to be mechanized; by the 1820s, factories on both sides of the Atlantic were producing cloth mechanically. As lucrative opportunities for textile production opened up, the industry was horrifically altered, particularly with regard to cotton. Throughout the late nineteenth and early twentieth centuries, Indigenous communities across North America and other parts of the world were violently displaced by colonial powers. The large tracts of land that had been stolen from them were populated with slaves who were forced to labor on cotton plantations. Europeans harnessed the forces of capitalism to create a global production complex that relied on the theft of land and human beings and used it to make themselves enormously wealthy while viciously denigrating Indigenous understandings of the earth that continue to hold nature as complex, sacred, and dominant. Rich countries in the West had learned to harness nature for commercial gain, and soon the market forces of consumerism would follow.

It was the fashion editor Diana Vreeland who said, "Fashion is part of the daily air, and it changes all the time, with all the events. You can even see the approaching of a revolution in clothes." That fashion reflects the mood of society is evident throughout history. The war years' aesthetic was severe and economical, but it was followed immediately by a post-war period in which men's suits took a V-shape in line with victory and Dior's 'New Look' saw women's hemlines fall twelve inches. As the woman's movement took off in the 1960s, Mary Quant created the mini skirt, raising hemlines and eyebrows as she centered youth as an economic force. Around the same time, Yves Saint Laurent created a men's black leather jacket made of crocodile and lined with mink. It was inspired by Marlon Brando and signaled that men could be objects of desire too.[6] By the 1970s, thirty-eight million women entered the work-force and started wearing trousers. A decade later came the economic boom of the 1980s, which celebrated supermodels and rock stars wear-ing fake fur under neon lights, the embodiment of hyperreal glamour.

By the 1990s, the recession had arrived. Corinne Day put Kate Moss, bright-eyed and elf-like, on the cover of *The Face* magazine. The shoot would launch Moss's career and set up the grunge movement that defined the '90s. It was a time synonymous with bare skin and bold silhouettes, clean lines and textured fabrics. A time when photographers like Day and Nan Goldin rebelled against the glossiness of high fashion and sought to express something real. Stylists would trawl thrift stores looking for vintage finds that could be twisted and customized to better tell a story about who someone really was. It was a time when anyone who loved fashion embraced newness and self-expression by altering and tailoring things themselves (a trend now resurfacing in DIY Tik-Toks and Instagram posts). There was individuality on the streets, when fabric was expensive and clothes cost what they should. They were an investment of money or energy or time, and it showed.

Globalization and the shift toward freer trade laws in the late 1990s and early 2000s changed all of that. Wave after wave of new technology, from methods of production to social media, have seen fashion arrive at a place where clothes cost almost nothing, are worn and loved less, but are purchased more. Prior to January 2005, two major trade agreements regulated the international textile market – the Multi Fiber Arrangement (MFA, 1974–1994) and the Agreement on Textiles and Clothing (ATC, 1995–2005). The MFA imposed quotas on the export of textiles and garments made from wool, cotton, and synthetic fibers from developing to developed countries. These quotas were designed to protect fashion houses in developed countries from low-cost goods produced en masse in developing countries. In 1995, the ATC agreed to encourage free trade and phase out quotas on trade in clothing and textiles; this was done by January 2005. In the four years following, one-third more clothing was consumed per capita.

The result is an industry that produces clothes so cheap it costs less to buy something new than have something old repaired, and unfortunately, the quality of some items may be so poor that repairs aren't even possible. It wasn't always like this. Headlines and advertisements in women's magazines from the 1950s and '60s reveal an attitude toward clothing that was very different from the dominant one today. One ad for wool sweaters reads, "Made to be washed. The more you wash it the better it is!" and another says, "These frocks look like new after four years' wear!"[7] The articles expressed things such as, "There's fashion and value in a wool coat. You need a wool coat this winter because wool gives you greater and longer wearability," and ask "Does your skirt keep its shape?"[8]

It didn't take long for the acceleration of fashion to infiltrate the upper echelons, with luxury brands turning to mass production to meet the demands of their ever-expanding customer base and projections for growth, which were no longer satiated by a mere two collections a year – the calendar and collective desire for newness demanded four or five. In 2010, Karl Lagerfeld, the creative director of Chanel, one of the most revered luxury houses in the world, said, "We are not in the old days, with two couture collections a year. At Chanel, we have six ready-to-wear collections."[9] But not everyone shared his enthusiasm, and other leading industry figures began to speak out. In 2016, Paul Smith described "this absolute horrendous disease of greed and over-expansion and unnecessary, massive over-supply of product."[10] A few years later, Giorgio Armani would say that "the decline of the fashion system as we know it began when the luxury segment adopted the operating methods of fast fashion, mimicking the latter's endless delivery cycle in the hope of selling more, yet forgetting that luxury takes time, to be achieved and to be appreciated."[11]

With the arrival of COVID-19 in early 2020, the industry was forced to look inward and consider its modus operandi. The editor in chief of *Vogue Italia*, Emanuele Farneti, asked, "Do we still need to buy more clothes? Does it still make sense to fly 1000 people from one country to another to attend 15 fashion shows?" His comments came from isolation in Lombardy, a region that suffered one of the most severe outbreaks of the virus. The pandemic caused production to slow across fashion's supply chains, with the two early crisis points for the epidemic, Wuhan and Northern Italy, being major hubs of manufacturing. Factory closures impacted production and deliveries, while sliding consumer confidence and nationwide lockdowns forced the closure of retail stores.

By May 2020, The British Fashion Council had joined forces with the Council of Fashion Designers of America to write a manifesto that encouraged "brands, designers and retailers, who are used to fashion's fast, unforgiving pace, to slow down." The manifesto came after a group of designers including Dries Van Noten, Gabriela Hearst, and Thom Browne wrote an open letter pledging "less unnecessary product, less waste in fabrics and inventory and less travel."[12]

But by 2021, as the world continued to reckon with the coronavirus pandemic, having spent eighteen months at home in loungewear, a longing for something else emerged during socially distanced fashion weeks in Paris and New York. Its embodiment was the type of delicate dresses and wisps of silk georgette that should only be worn with high heels, jewelry, and soft perfumes. Upon seeing a plunging black silk-crepe dress with gold chain shoulder straps, journalist Alice Cavanagh wrote in the *Financial Times*: "An unfamiliar feeling ignited inside me. I wanted to put the dress on. And go out out. I wanted ... to feel sexy again. For months I had happily been hiding away in layer upon layer of comfort wear ... But then the news of the vaccine's arrival made the reality of going to a bar or restaurant, one day at least, a real possibility. Paris by night. God, how I miss you."[13] In an article for *The New York Times*, the writer Lou Stoppard fantasized about a party where her "feet hurt from impractical shoes – maybe heels, maybe some kind of heavy, embellished boot. I wave across the room at an acquaintance, and my stacks of bracelets bang against one another, distracting me momentarily from the pinching of an elaborately engineered strapless bra that I will pre-emptively unhook in the taxi home. How I long for such discomfort."[14]

When asked about what would happen to fashion after the pandemic, the designer Tom Ford said, "What happened after the Spanish flu? We had the Roaring Twenties. We had consumption and flappers and makeup and exuberance."[15]

The question is how to marry two desires that have until now worked in opposition to each other. The first is the desire to create a 'sustainable' fashion industry. The second is to create beautiful clothes that give us the ability to experience joy and express ourselves when we wear them. Of course, every pledge to rebuild supply chains and reconfigure the industry to be more sustainable is a welcome indication that fashion is ready to change. Hopefully that change will come in many, varied forms. The issues are complicated and pose incredible challenges that will require interdisciplinary collaboration across science and technology. But the techniques of the farm-to-table food movement give us an exciting place to start. By integrating the principles of regenerative agriculture into fashion's supply chains, we could create an industry that is truly sustainable. The key is driving positive outcomes for nature through the sourcing and farming of raw materials that produce beautiful clothes of a very high quality.

What's exciting about this type of farming is the speed at which it can turn landscapes around and its potential to affect broadscale positive change. Some farmers believe that with the right systems in place, degraded land can regenerate in just ten years. That land can then produce crops with more nutrients and a better ability to withstand extreme weather and pests. Plus, if we concentrate on developing healthy soils, we begin to capture the atmospheric carbon dioxide that's warming the planet and reverse some of the harm done by the last seventy years of farming.[16]

Healthy soils store more carbon than the atmosphere and vegetation combined.[17] Soil is the safest place to store the billions of tons of carbon dioxide that have already been released into the atmosphere. It is safer than the ocean because excess carbon dioxide can turn the water acidic and make it inhospitable to marine life. It is safer than trees and plants because when trees and plants die and decompose, or burn in wildfires, the carbon is released back into the atmosphere. Soils can store carbon for decades, for millennia, forever.

While this is all extremely exciting, the science on carbon sequestration is still evolving, and there is a lack of consensus about the mechanisms of long-term carbon storage. This is why carbon credits and the carbon market, and brands claiming to offset their carbon footprints, should be treated with skepticism. Carbon sequestration and the positive effects of carbon-rich soil should be viewed as one piece of the puzzle. A 2022 report released by Textile Exchange calls for the industry to do its due diligence before making claims about greenhouse gas reductions and not to lose sight of big the picture – restoring the health of the landscapes along their supply chain.[18]

Nevertheless, the promise of regenerative agriculture is thrilling because it's not just about survival in the face of doom-and-gloom predictions about the fate of the earth. It's about a return to the breathtaking wilderness that caused humanity to worship the earth for centuries. A dramatic re-wilding, a return to the "morning that had once throbbed with the dawn chorus of robins, catbirds, doves, jays, wrens, and scores of other bird voices," as described by Rachel Carson in her seminal work *Silent Spring*.[19] The question is, how?

There are many pioneers of this approach who have married ecological systems-thinking with modern land management and scientific knowledge. In interviews with more than one hundred regenerative farmers, Charles Massy found a common theme emerged: nature will drive it for you if you get out of the way.[20]

According to Gabe Brown, the author of *Dirt to Soil*, the basic principles of regenerative farming have been developed by nature over eons (something Indigenous communities have always known). His starting point is no-till or minimal intervention, which means limiting disturbance of the soil. This allows the soil to build in a way that improves water infiltration. When the soil efficiently absorbs and stores water, it makes the landscape more resilient to changing weather patterns and periods of drought.[21]

Another principle is to keep the soil covered with plant life or mulch at all times. Sometimes this involves planting cover crops after the main crop is harvested to protect the soil from wind and water erosion, replenish nutrients that might have been lost in the previous crop, foster macro- and micro-organisms, and prevent the germination of weed seeds. Cover cropping also helps to maintain living roots in the soil for as long as possible, which is important because roots feed the soil with carbon, which in turn feeds the plants and makes them more nutritious.

Without an active root network, soil can become like sand, making it vulnerable to erosion.

Ensuring diversity in plants also attracts beneficial insects that can protect crops from predator insects in the place of pesticides and insecticides. This multi-species planting can include inter- or alley-cropping, where crops are planted in alternating rows; pollinator strips of flowering plants interspersed with hero crops to attract pollinator insects; and trees and shrubs to encourage birds and wildlife.

The integration of livestock can also benefit plants because, when grazed by animals, the plants are stimulated to pump more carbon into the soil. A plant considers a bite by an animal to be a wound, which requires a healing process. The plant needs nutrients to heal and sets to work collecting them by releasing substances to attract and feed carbon-hungry microbes. This type of herbivore grazing needs to be managed so the herds are constantly moving and are not allowed to exhaust a paddock by overgrazing it. The concept is based on the work of French farmer André Voisin and has been advanced by Allan Savory, who observed wild herbivores and sought to mimic their relationship with the land.

Of course, implementing these systems takes time. Farmers must account for the rhythms of the seasons and the dynamics of distinct ecosystems, things that vary across farms, landscapes, and continents. But the hope is that, eventually, when some of these elements have been activated, nature will once again take over, and the inherent power and capacity of natural systems will return with heightened intricacy, strength, and resilience. According to Massy, embracing regenerative systems requires farmers to have some humility and acknowledge "the inherent self-organizing capacity of natural ecosystems and other complex dynamic systems."[22]

This humility and deference to nature has always been at the heart of Indigenous approaches to land management, and today, Native communities and communities of color are essential to regenerative farming. Robin Wall Kimmerer describes how "in Native ways of knowing, human people are referred to as the 'younger brothers of Creation.'" We must look to our teachers among the other species for guidance. Their wisdom is apparent in the way that they live. They teach us by example. They've been on the earth far longer than we have been and have had time to figure things out."[23]

It takes two hours and twenty-five minutes to get to the bearded farmer's property, a 370-acre vineyard northwest of Melbourne. On the farm, he has one hundred acres of grapes and an acre of fruit trees, including mulberries, peaches, figs, and apples. The area was touted by the European colonizers as the food bowl of Victoria, but he says that when this assessment was made, "they didn't really see the cycles of the place."

He describes the landscape as typically Australian: stark and bare. In the summer, some of the eucalypts become scraggly while other areas remain densely forested. These parts are protected national park since they contain original bush scrub. The region has seen more than two centuries of sheep grazing and when they took over the farm, the property had no topsoil.

Initially, his father and uncle tried to rebuild it using mid-row cover cropping through the vineyard, but when the plants reached maturity, they would rip them up and spray the base of the vines with the herbicide Roundup. After a decade of operating this way, they'd made little progress. The earth was still hard. The crop yields were low. They were forced to change tack.

The bearded farmer decided to let weeds come up among the vines instead, and allowed the mid-row crops to mature, die, and fall back into the soil. He stopped spraying synthetics and started planting tillage radishes along the mid-row to aerate the soil and add nutrients. He also layered mulch and compost beneath the vines. All of this helped the soil retain moisture and increase fungal matter, so an "incredible humus layer started to evolve" – just because of the small layer of protection being added on top. He left acres and acres of depleted grasslands alone and, eventually, they came back to life. Thanks to a natural seed bank that had reserves deep underground, groves of eucalypts keep emerging.

The contrast to the neighboring farms still running sheep and spraying synthetics could not be starker: their properties are so scarred by erosion you can see it from the road. "What you really see, when the summer comes, is that our place stays greener longer, where a lot of other places around us go brown really quick," he says.

Compared to the farm's dry and dusty beginnings, when it "was just so blisteringly hot and everything was very hard," the bearded farmer says, now the land feels "naturally abundant." It is home to a huge array of native wildlife and birds that were not there two decades ago. "God, I saw a quail the other day when I woke up," he says, "and there was a swarm of bees holed up on top of one of the posts to the vineyard, which I had never seen before." The land is also supporting kangaroos, wedge-tailed eagles, and owls. "There is a natural corridor of forest that runs through the property, so that brings a lot of things through. But enabling those smaller groves of eucalypt to grow back – that is where you are seeing the native species return."

Perhaps the most interesting thing from a holistic management perspective is the fruit the land is producing. Parts of the vineyard are producing now that never produced before. "And producing really good fruit," the farmer says. "It is astounding." He describes how, in three short years, yields on a section that had been notoriously difficult have increased from half a ton per acre to one and a half tons per acre. It has improved in both quality and quantity: "It is better than when we were using synthetics."

I have tasted apples from that orchard and wine from the vineyard and seen the farmer carry boxes of fruit from the farm into restaurants (including his own). In so many ways, the farm-to-table movement is more straightforward than the farm-to-closet: an apple does not undergo the many stages of processing required for cotton or wool to be wearable; in fact, it can be eaten straight from the tree. But the principles of regenerative farming are transferable, from growing peaches, figs, and grapes to growing cotton, flax, wool, cashmere, hemp, and even silk. The landscapes where fibers are being farmed in a way that heals ecosystems and gives back to nature are spread all over the world – some on a smaller or larger scale than the bearded farmer's, and most with complicated relationships to processing and production. But regardless, the same cycles of biology apply, transforming sunlight into plant matter we can harvest, spin, and weave, turning it into beautiful clothes we get to wear against our skin. Clothes that give back to the earth. Clothes that allow us to be *sundressed.*

CHAPTER 3
A Shirt Made of Flowers

I watch a waiter move between the tables. He is wearing blue jeans and a white singlet underneath a crisp white cotton shirt. He wears the shirt open with the sleeves rolled to his elbows. The fabric is taut across his shoulders, so it hangs easily through the body. It is a cool autumn morning, and the sun casts soft shadows through the trees onto the outdoor tables and glasses of water, across plates of figs and honey, buttered toast, hard cheese, and soft-boiled eggs. We could be anywhere in the world. I know the waiter owns the café/wine bar. I have heard stories of his obsessive attention to detail and particular ways of running his business. There is an enormous tear-shaped beaker of apple cider vinegar fermenting on an old oak shelf inside the door and large jars of preserved lemons, pickled chilies, and sweet tomatoes on a ledge high above the kitchen. The beauty of this place can be distracting but today, I am distracted by his shirt and how perfect it can be to wear something as simple as white cotton.

In 2012, Rei Kawakubo, the creative director of Comme des Garçons, told a journalist, "I would have liked to invent the plain white shirt."[1] Coming from a woman widely considered one of the most artistic people in the fashion industry, this confession is revealing. Over centuries, the white shirt has, at different times, been a symbol of both androgyny and intellectualism. Throughout the Renaissance, it was worn as an undergarment, until 1779, when Marie Antoinette was painted wearing it as outerwear. Ernest Hemingway wore a white shirt with the collar unbuttoned and the sleeves hiked up while he wrote *For Whom the Bell Tolls*. His friend F. Scott Fitzgerald wore his white shirts with neck ties and high-waisted pants. In the 1930s, the white shirt was picked up by Hollywood, when society was changing, and masculine and feminine ideals became things that could be played with. The film star Marlene Dietrich, who challenged perceptions of gender, wore soft white shirts with her pleat-front pantsuits. She was famously quoted as saying, "I dress for the image. Not for myself, not for the public, not for fashion, not for men." Audrey Hepburn ran around Rome in a white shirt with a popped collar and rolled-up sleeves in *Roman Holiday* in 1953; alongside her, Gregory Peck had one on beneath his suit. In stark contrast to the feminine dresses she was usually seen in, Marilyn Monroe wore a sleeveless white shirt with blue jeans in the 1961 film *The Misfits*.

Throughout the 1960s, James Baldwin seemed to wear a white shirt almost all of the time, including during his famous debate at Cambridge. Sitting in front of a packed bookshelf, Susan Sontag wore a white shirt while she smoked and tapped away on her typewriter. In 1975, Patti Smith wore a white shirt on the cover of her album *Horses* and confessed to *The New York Times* that the outfit was inspired by the French poet Baudelaire. From 1975 to 1976, David Bowie performed as the Thin White Duke, a controversial character who always wore a white shirt, black trousers, and a waistcoat. Jean-Michel Basquiat wore an oversized white shirt with baggy white jeans and high-top sneakers while painting the *Gold Griot* in 1984. In 1988, fashion photographer Peter Lindbergh photographed a group of models (including Linda Evangelista and Christy Turlington) on a Santa Monica beach wearing crisp white shirts and nothing else. The photos were scrapped by the American *Vogue* editor who had commissioned them, only to be discovered and printed four years later by the new editor-in-chief, Anna Wintour.

Some estimates date the use of cotton as far back as seven thousand years. It has been found in ruins across Iraq, Greece, China, and Northern Africa, and for long stretches of history it has been one of the most important agricultural commodities in the world. Its trade has underpinned the technological developments of manufacturing industries from Manchester to China. At the end of the eighteenth century, it played a critical role in the advancement of colonialism and the industrial revolution. Both forces changed the way cotton was grown and manufactured, as imperial expansion aligned with the slave trade and the invention of mechanized textile production systems. Cotton became a means of separating the dispossessors and the dispossessed, the colonizers and the colonized.[2]

In recent years, conventional cotton farming has been maligned by people inside and outside the fashion industry as environmentally costly. It causes a myriad of ecological issues, including pollution of soil, waterways, and airways by pesticides and synthetic fertilizers. Cotton is often planted as a monocrop, which exacerbates the need for both chemicals and causes widespread degradation of the soil. Degraded soil has terrible water retention and requires extensive irrigation, which brings us to cotton's most infamous quality – its water use. If cotton is being harvested in areas where the supply of water is insufficient, water needs to be pumped to the cultivation site, and doing so often requires machinery that can cause soil erosion.[3] Additionally, when water flow is diverted to irrigate cotton plants, it can stress natural water reserves and deplete groundwater tables, rivers, and lakes. The Aral Sea shrank to a tenth of its original size due in large part to cotton irrigation.

These facts are whirling around in my head while my friend Caroline and I drive to a cotton farm in Central Queensland. The long gold road stretches out ahead of us. We cross flat expanses of farmland where we cannot see a single tree, where the rows of soil look dry and dusty, where the sun feels unforgiving. Eventually the empty paddocks and fields give way to woodland inhabited by varied species of native grasses with feathery red tips and golden stems. In places, the grass is so tall, it meets the lowest branches of the gray-green eucalypts, so it looks as though the tops of the trees are floating on grass clouds. The air feels softer, and the fading sunshine casts pretty orange light across the dashboard. Soon we'll stop so we can have dinner and sleep, then we'll continue on our way in the morning. I tell Caroline that the farm we're visiting is "on its way to being regenerative," but that I'm not entirely sure what that means because cotton farming is widely considered thirsty, resource-hungry, and polluting.

As we drive the expansive roads into Glenn Rogan's farm, we notice more changes in the landscape. There are long tracks of water that run the borders of each paddock; his cotton plants are taller and wider than the others we'd driven past – we decide they look *fat*. Caroline winds down her window to say hello to a scruffy Jack Russell approaching the car to greet us. Rogan's cheerful wife, Julianne, welcomes us into the kitchen and makes us coffee before he arrives wearing a wide cream Akubra hat and a cobalt-blue shirt that I'm certain he knows make his blue eyes brighter. He hands me a cotton boll on a small branch. Caroline and I are mesmerized. We pull apart the soft, white fibers and send them floating into the air.

This fluffy white ball that forms around the seeds has been bred across millennia to be bigger so it produces more fiber.[4] After harvest, the fiber is separated from the seeds at a cotton gin. The seeds are captured and used in vegetable oil or cattle feed and the cotton fiber is sold in bales to processors who turn the bales into yarn. They begin by using a machine to card it into a long, wide strip to align the fibers and pull them into a loose rope. It then goes through several more stages of pulling and spinning to smooth and strengthen the fibers until, eventually, it becomes a thin yarn. The length of the cotton's fibers, or staples, will dictate its quality: longer staples produce higher quality, smoother textiles.

Cotton crops require at least 150 days of sunshine and are grown in warm climates all over the world, usually within thirty-five degrees latitude of the equator. Cotton is planted in the spring in long, straight rows. On our farm tour a little later on, Rogan will explain that the seeds they plant are genetically modified (GM) Bollgard seeds. He says since they started using GM seeds, they have reduced their pesticides by ninety-five percent.

My knowledge of GM seeds is largely from the impact they had on India's cotton industry. When the genetically modified Bt cotton variety was introduced in 2002, it quickly spread across the country, and within a decade, it made up ninety-five percent of India's cotton production. The modification enabled the plant to produce the Bt protein, which kills cotton's major pests – heliothis and the cotton bollworm – and in theory, requires fewer harmful pesticides. GM seeds are expensive and must be purchased every year, which is a change from traditional farming, where seeds are saved from the previous year's crop. Despite this, because the seeds are designed to reduce pesticide use, it was thought they would save the farmers money in the long term and make cotton farming safer. Unfortunately, the insects grew resistant, and farmers found themselves buying more pesticides in addition to the seeds. In a cruel twist, the price of cotton dropped, and farmers began to complain of lower yields. The combination of rising costs and diminished returns trapped them in a cycle of sky-rocketing debt. Heartbreakingly, cotton farmers across India began to commit suicide at alarming rates, often by drinking pesticides.[5]

In Australia, the use of GM seeds is regulated. Rogan tells me you have to plant a refuge crop to manage susceptible insects and prevent resistant moths from mating with each other – because resistance is a recessive trait, if you control which moths mate, you can prevent resistant offspring from being born. To do this, they "switch from one chemistry to another, kill a caterpillar or the egg of a caterpillar, never put the same spray on, or apply the same spray in a different lifecycle of the caterpillar." He shows me a field that was planted with organic cotton (part of the resistance-management plan) and tells me that, out of the ten years they've planted organic cotton, it's only once yielded enough cotton to harvest. To achieve the yields they get from GM cotton, they'd need ten times the land and ten times the water, making it commercially unviable. In a dry country like Australia, farmers need to decide how can they make the most money with the water they are allocated and take the best care of their land, which is why Rogan is still spraying some chemicals and working with GM seeds, neither of which are regenerative techniques.

But he is persisting with other ways to build nutrients in the soil and reduce his reliance on chemicals. He has introduced alley-cropping to his fields so rows of cotton are alternated with rows of mung beans and pigeon pea. He rotates paddocks, also growing corn and wheat depending on the season and their water allocations. Farming is full of dilemmas like this, dilemmas that extend beyond ideals to the reality of working the land, especially when there are not necessarily clear answers as the regenerative fiber farming movement is still just beginning.

Genetically modified cotton now makes up around seventy-five percent of the global cotton crop.[6] In the United States, it represents around ninety-four percent of the cotton grown, and in Australia ninety-nine percent. It is so widespread that, when Rebecca Burgess began her trials of farming climate-beneficial cotton in California, she couldn't get access to seeds that didn't have the genetic modification.

Burgess lives on a 200-acre ranch, about an hour from the San Joaquin Valley. In addition to hosting a cow-calf operation, the ranch is an organic food production site where they also farm fiber, dye, and medicine. Among the many rows of crops, Burgess has indigo, marigolds, and flax. She trained as a weaver and natural dyer before she founded an organization called Fibershed out of a "need to heal these working landscapes." She speaks with a lightness and ease, but there is tension behind her words – as though the enormity and importance of the work she has taken on doesn't disappear despite the wild beauty of where she lives and the hope her work affords the fashion industry. Kate Fletcher has described her work as "bold, practical, optimistic – a vision of how things must be." Her love of nature feels tangible; while we are speaking, she comes across a dead baby bird outside the ranch and her distress is evident. "So precious, so tiny – her eyes aren't even open yet, sweet thing," she says, her voice wavering with emotion, before she resolves: "I'm going to bury her, for sure."

Fibershed is a non-profit organization dedicated to bringing back local, healthy methods of growing and manufacturing fiber, from wool to hemp and cotton. The movement has pioneered the idea of climate-beneficial fiber, from "soil to skin." Natural fibers and dyes are grown using carbon-farming practices and then processed into garments using renewable energy within a 500-mile radius. The result is garments with a carbon-neutral or carbon-negative footprint.

Fibershed is currently piloting a suite of carbon-farming practices in cotton agriculture – in other words, methods of sequestering carbon in the soil. They include regenerative agriculture techniques designed to improve soil health – like no-tilling, multi-species cover cropping, and eliminating the use of pesticides and synthetic fertilizers – and some that are more specific to cotton growing, like fungal compost systems. These methods rebuild organic matter and soil microbes, increase the soil's ability to hold water, and alleviate pest pressure.

One of Burgess's long-time collaborators is California farmer Sally Fox. Fox lives in an agricultural valley near Sacramento and is famous for growing colored cottons. They have become increasingly rare due to the industry's preference for long-staple white cotton that is easy to spin and dye. She also runs a farm that is certified organic and biodynamic, and her cotton has been verified by Fibershed as climate-beneficial. She uses a variety of techniques to increase the carbon content in her soil, including rotating wheat with cotton, integrated grazing of Merino sheep, and planting black-eyed peas alongside her cotton. In addition to improving soil health, the peas double as a trap to lure pests away from the cotton. The sheep provide natural fertilizer with their dung and urine. She doesn't use pesticides or synthetic fertilizers, and she only needs to water her cotton once a fortnight. She has the data to prove that her practices sequester atmospheric carbon. In collaboration with Fibershed and the Gaudin Lab at the University of California, Fox has been tracking her soil's carbon levels, and the findings show the soil's organic matter has increased from 1 to 2.6 percent.

Not far from Sally Fox's farm – at the Center for Regenerative Agriculture and Resilient Systems at California State University, Chico – another Fibershed collaborator is researching ways for cotton farming to benefit the climate. Dr. David Johnson is exploring the use of fungal-dominated compost extracts and multi-species cover cropping to biologically enhance the soil, sequester carbon, and improve crop yields. His research has found that when you increase the ratio of fungi to bacteria in the soil, plants absorb nutrients more efficiently and are more productive as a result. This means fungi could be more significant than nitrogen, phosphorous, potassium, or even organic matter. Johnson has created a composting system that allows fungi to develop over a year; the structure lets the soil aerate, and worms help to foster species diversity in the compost, mimicking those in healthy soil ecosystems.[7] The compost can be spread over the top of the soil or used to coat the seeds prior to planting. Inoculating the seeds with microbes allows them to germinate more quickly and boosts growth. The approach also includes the integration of livestock when practical. Johnson's cotton test-run grew taller than normal cotton plants and produced more than five bales of cotton per acre without fertilizers or pesticides – roughly double the normal yields for the area. During an agricultural field study lasting four and a half years, he documented a twenty-five-fold increase in active soil fungi and an annual average capture of approximately 38,000 pounds of carbon per acre.[8] He believes it was so successful because of the importance of restoring fungal populations to the biological life of the soil.

According to Burgess, Johnson's work indicates that supporting healthy microbes makes crops more productive and better able to store water and withstand drought. But she goes on to say that after running some further trials, they realized the "method needs to be modified per bio-region" because Johnson hadn't proved that the cotton he harvested was able to be milled, and his crop was planted too late in the season for commercial purposes. Overall, though, she says it is "on the right track."[9]

Another issue with growing cotton in California is defoliation, the process of stripping the cotton plant of its leaves to make harvesting more efficient. In an organic process, a drop in temperature would cause the leaves to freeze and fall off the plant naturally, but in California, where the climate is always temperate, this doesn't happen. In Queensland, Rogan applies an herbicide called Dropp to remove the leaves. Without it, he says, they would have to run the cotton picker through the fields twice, expending more energy to remove the excess leaves and debris from the cotton. For Burgess, this poses a dilemma as the Fibershed program is dedicated to making sure farmers don't have to rely on buying chemicals; the systems have to be both economically and ecologically regenerative. This underscores the struggle she has with genetically modified seeds – the need to repurchase them every year means the economic model is not truly regenerative. From an ecological perspective, she tells me, most GM seeds have been treated with fungicides, "so you're putting these biology-killing treatments on the seeds and then you're planting them and you're expecting good results for the ecology and the soil biology." For the pilot with David Johnson, they had to use GM seeds because they couldn't access an alternative, so they left out the herbicide and fungicide and coated them with the compost from Johnson's bioreactor instead.

Burgess acknowledges the complexities of balancing expectations for organic crops with the realities of harvesting something to create a desirable product. She says the use of precious resources in cotton farming might only be justified if we grow less, do so thoughtfully, and only use virgin cotton for very high-end garments. She acknowledges it might sound elitist but says that from an environmental perspective, it's very egalitarian: "If you're a soil microbe or a migratory bird or an earthworm, you'll say, thank you, humans, please pay five dollars a pound for your cotton, give me a break and stop killing me."

In 2021, the United Nations Fashion Industry Charter for Climate Action released a report called "Identifying Low Carbon Sources of Cotton and Polyester Fibers." Its findings were in line with the Fibershed approaches, highlighting the need to phase out synthetic fertilizers and increase on-farm composting in order to reduce emissions from cotton agriculture. Burgess and I talk about the difficulty of convincing conventional farmers, who have spent their whole lives believing in and applying synthetic fertilizers, to change. Their understanding of soil health is rooted in the idea that farming removes nutrients from the soil and, by applying fertilizer, they are helping it. "It's so interesting to think that, if I put this in the soil, as a *Homo sapiens*, then I am doing good for the soil because I'm giving it something," Burgess says. She argues we need to shift our understanding because nitrogen is in the air and the trick to getting it into the soil is to "find plants that can help us capture it from the air." She tells me, "I love my plants, I always want to give them an input. Can I water you? Can I give you compost tea?" But she understands that usually plants don't need anything, except for the right crop rotation. "You don't have to keep handing them cupcakes to keep them happy. No more synthetic nitrates – you're killing them, you're giving them diabetes."

Fibershed is running several other pilot programs that are working to find creative ways to make farming cotton climate-beneficial. She describes farmers who use sunflower and alfalfa strips as hero crops, and an agroforestry program that plants mulberry and fig trees in wide rows with cotton running in between. She is keen to impress on me the need to take a season-by-season, year-by-year, region-by-region approach. "Does it work every year, different rain pattern, different wind pattern, different snow melt? All these different conditions absolutely change things, like insect pressure. You've got to do it thoughtfully." Her comments are both gentle and piercingly insightful. "We've invested money in blunt tools, and we've disinvested our communities to be observers of nature," she says. "I am trying to be guided by an approach instead of a recipe."

Part of this approach is to transform fashion's international, disparate supply chains that are often so complicated that even the best textile suppliers can't tell you where their raw materials originated. Burgess believes in a localized manufacturing system and a return of infrastructure that connects farmers to consumers, where everything is traceable, where no chemicals are involved, and all the energy used is clean. More than 200,000 acres of cotton are grown in the San Joaquin Valley – enough for everyone in the state of California to have seven pairs of jeans made for them. But, Burgess says, "we have no manufacturing." Instead, California imports most of its clothing. She wants to see the system change so that people take responsibility for their textile culture, develop efficient renewable energy–powered manufacturing systems close to where fiber and dyes are grown, and "really try to build partnerships and an organizational structure that allows us to have 'soil to skin and back to soil,' all in one bio-region." She wants to develop regional systems of diverse communities that honor ancestral connections to land and techniques. Ultimately, she hopes to empower makers to cherish and use the skills and craftsmanship that used to be passed between generations.

The first time Angel Chang flew into Guizhou province, it was like entering a dreamscape. As the plane began its descent, the air turned soft and fuzzy. When the land below came into view, she could see a vast mountain range covered in dense forest. After disembarking, she and her small entourage, which included a translator to navigate the language barrier and a driver to navigate the winding roads and foreign terrain, drove ten hours to a village where (she had been told) people still had the skills to make the traditional textiles and costumes of the region. Until that day, she had only been exposed to the costumes and fabrics in museums and galleries, but it was their beauty and the promise of a connection to her cultural heritage that had brought her so far from New York. And here were people wearing them, working the lush green fields of Guizhou, as though time had stopped one hundred years before and the technological advancements of consumer-driven globalization had never happened.

Angel Chang's eponymous womenswear line is handmade by the Indigenous mountain tribes of Guizhou province. They use ancient techniques to grow cotton, silk, and dyes that follow the cycles of nature. Over a decade, Chang worked closely with the fabric masters who passed down their techniques from mother to daughter and built a regional supply chain to create an entire collection of garments sourced from raw materials that had been grown within a thirty-mile radius.

Chang started her career working for Donna Karan and says when she moved to Guizhou in 2012, she had to "forget everything she had been trained to do as a fashion designer in New York." She wanted to create a line of clothing using techniques humans had relied on throughout history – without chemicals or electricity. To do so, she had to change her understanding of time. In nature, it was not possible to produce fabric in any color at any time of year: the climate dictated what would grow, and so the seasons would dictate when her collection could be produced. Globalization had changed the economic model of the province and, instead of staying to work the land and learn the traditions of their ancestors, the younger generations were leaving Guizhou to work in factories. Skills and craftsmanship that had survived over centuries were disappearing, and finding people who still had knowledge of ancient techniques like spinning and weaving became a "race against time." After three years of searching, she finally found some grandmothers who knew how to spin cotton by hand.

The Miao and Dong tribes that call Guizhou province home grow native seed cotton from April to August on small family farms. Chang tells me they each have "one mu of land," or roughly one-sixth of an acre. On this land, they grow everything they need to survive, including mulberry trees to feed their silkworms. "In the summer, it's cotton; at other times, it's soybeans and spinach – whatever they need to eat."

In the province, it rains every three days, so the cotton can grow without irrigation, and the villagers don't apply pesticides or synthetic fertilizers. Chang is opposed to using GM cotton; she says her cotton uses less water and doesn't require chemicals because it's native to the land. There are only three ingredients in her collection: plants, sun, and mountain water.

The fabrics – which are all cotton – are hand-spun, hand-woven, washed in mountain water, dried in the sun, and softened by being pounded against stones with wooden mallets. As Chang explains the limitations of using natural dyes, I can feel her longing for the bright hues and solid blacks that were accessible in her previous life in New York. "I can't dye every color in the rainbow. Geographically, you only have access to certain colors in different regions of the world. We don't have bright red. For that, we'd have to go to Mexico; for turquoise, you have to go to Tibet." They have to rely on whatever plants are in their region. Indigo grows wild in Guizhou province. In May, they harvest the fallen petals of the buddleia flowers from the forest floor to make a soft yellow; they use red soil to create a soft clay color; and in August, they forage gardenia pods to make a bright yellow. Each garment is cut and sewn entirely by hand, so the investment of time is significant: a jacket takes ten days, a dress takes six, a pair of pants takes four. Dyeing can take up to two weeks, depending on the humidity levels. Electricity in the village is unreliable, so the locals mostly live a traditional agrarian lifestyle – everything is powered by sunlight, firewood, water buffalo, or their own hands. The model has limitations for a commercial brand: the pieces are expensive (a shirt costs US$875), and Chang can only make one collection a year, in contrast to the usual four to six of big luxury brands. She is rightly unapologetic about the cost, and when people ask why her clothes are so expensive, she says, "Well, you spend thirty days weaving that."*

The first garment she tried to make with the artisans was a shirt. She decided that recreating a classic button-down would be their first test. The final product is a white, long-sleeve shirt with a drop shoulder and a relaxed fit though the body. She shortened the length to make it more feminine and easier to pair with high-waisted trousers. The buttons are intricate beads of fabric, made using the ancient technique of hand-knotting cotton cording, so everything is from the land and can return to it. Chang quantifies the time required for each piece: this shirt

---

* Chang uses a standard markup to price her garments, meaning the cost price of an $850 shirt is approximately $212.50, which includes the cost of fabric and labor.

takes between five and six months from cotton seed to finished product. The cotton takes four months to grow, and then it takes three days to clean it and prepare it for spinning. Hand spinning takes five days. Setting up the loom takes a week. The hand weaving takes three to five days. It takes a day to cut the fabric and at least three days to sew it, plus another two to wash it. The result is a shirt so soft, it has an easy drape through the body. It is made from undyed cotton, so it has basically come directly off the plant, and Chang tells me it is as close as you can get to wearing something straight from the earth.

I think about this the next time I pull on a shirt. I think about how the cotton feels against my skin, light and soft. I think about how much I like to wear one after a shower because of the way it absorbs moisture. I think about the holidays I've been on when a shirt was enough to throw on over a swimsuit, to shield against the sun and the wind, and how, because cotton can be washed at high temperatures, the fabric was never ruined by salt from the sea or the residue of sunscreen. I think about Audrey Hepburn wandering through her bare New York apartment in *Breakfast at Tiffany's* in nothing but a men's tuxedo shirt and a blue eye mask and wonder what it is about cotton that makes the white shirt so enduring.

As awareness of fashion's environmental footprint has increased, cotton has become the industry's most maligned fabric. Burgess describes it as a "whipping post for the entire fiber system" and in many ways, she's right. When I told people I was going to visit a cotton farm, the typical response was that cotton is notoriously bad. Some of this criticism is fair – throughout history, cotton farming and cultivation have caused people and landscapes enormous pain, and this pain is still being inflicted in many places. But the scrutiny directed at cotton is disproportionate when its environmental footprint is compared to other fabrics, and it always overshadows the fact that cotton is an incredible crop.

Cotton comes off the plant white and fluffy and ready to be spun into yarn. After harvesting, it requires no water or chemicals until the dying stage of processing. When we compare its raw state to that of viscose or polyester, it seems insane that we consider it to be more environmentally costly. Viscose begins as a tree, and even if you can get past the environmental implications of cutting down a forest to make a collection, the process of converting wood into a smooth and silky textile is wild: it requires enormous amounts of chemicals and wastes most of the tree. Polyester is a common plastic derived from fossilized carbon and yet, to the disbelief of many sustainable fashion advocates and experts, cotton has been ranked as having a worse environmental impact than polyester by the Sustainable Apparel Coalition's Higg Material Sustainability Index – a rating tool widely relied on by designers and fashion businesses. This is in part due to a lack of consensus about the metrics for determining environmental impact. For instance, polyester's rating does not account for the emissions released during extraction of the raw material; it disregards the impact of drilling or fracking of fossil fuels to create polyester and instead calculates its environmental impact from when the material is in pellet form.[10] It also states that its water use is significantly less than cotton's, when other studies estimate it is actually seven times higher.[11] Plus, Higg relies on standardized data collected from the industry, which can be much harder for smaller farms, like Indigenous farmers in the hills of Guizhao, to collect and provide. Understandably, for some experts this is a problematic way to set up life cycle assessments (LCAs) because it oversimplifies the metrics for complicated processes. According to Rebecca Burgess, nuance is critical for LCAs of cotton because calculations need to account for differences in ecosystems across regions. The organic carbon level of the soil, for instance, can vary even across the same field. To paint all conventional cotton or organic cotton with the same brush, or to use one LCA for the cotton from a whole country, is to eradicate the nuance and complexity that is necessary to properly understand the environmental impact of the fiber. She describes the Higg methodology as so blunt as to be "unscientific."

I think about this in the context of Glenn Rogan's farming. He introduced me to an important calculation that the sustainable fashion movement sometimes overlooks, which is to measure carbon emissions based on a yield-per-inputs ratio. For instance, if organic cotton requires ten times the land and ten times the water to achieve the same yields as conventional cotton, is it really better for the environment? There's not enough information to determine the impact of a genetically modified cotton seed on the health of the soil but, hypothetically, according to Rogan's metrics, best-practice cotton farming involves maximizing your yield per units of water while maintaining soil health. For him, this means choosing GM seeds to dramatically reduce pesticide use, employing alley-cropping, cover crops, and crop rotations to improve nitrogen in the soil and applying Dropp to defoliate the plants before picking to produce a clean fiber that requires minimal processing. If we apply Burgess's reasoning to the equation, we can say this might be what works in his particular region, in Queensland, where water is scarce. His farm is on a river and his water use is highly regulated, as is the way he uses GM seeds. While he admits his process is not perfect, he is committed to improving the quality of his soil and reducing the farm's reliance on chemicals – as long as he can balance his inputs with his outputs.

When we consider Angel Chang's cotton, the calculation is different again, and her approach is hard to fault. It rains every three days in her region, so the cotton requires no irrigation, and the farmers don't use fertilizers, pesticides, or defoliants – but they also only grow enough cotton for one of her collections per year, so her garments are exceptionally rare and expensive, putting them out of reach for most people. While limiting supply would help reduce fashion's environmental footprint, there is work to be done to translate Chang's model on a broader scale. Setting up networks of regional economies that encourage connection to land and ancestral practices might be one way to do this. Already, networks of farmers across India (where half of the world's organic cotton is grown) are working with native seed cotton and collaborating with spinners, weavers, and dyers—providing an example of how to scale integrated regenerative farming and heirloom manufacturing processes.

Ultimately, these unanswered questions are the reason why the work Burgess is doing in California is so important. By running different pilot programs, experimenting, and figuring out how to influence carbon levels in the soil while accounting for commercial yields and fiber quality, Fibershed is working to transform conventional cotton farming into a tool to regenerate ecosystems, landscapes, and the earth.

CHAPTER 4

La Dolce Vita and the Australian Merino

The first time I visited the Italian stylist's atelier, I was wearing a black oversized knit I'd bought in London. Paris Fashion Week had just finished, and I was hopeful she might offer me a job. I'd spent the evening before scouring her website and Instagram trying to figure out what to wear. There was one collection (or edition, as she preferred to call them) that was shot in the gritty and romantic capital of Sicily, Palermo. The images were arresting: black-and-white photos shot in direct sunlight. Each image was a moment, like the first morning of a holiday that begins with coffee in the middle of the afternoon. The model's hair was unbrushed. The clothes looked both lived-in and fresh. The details of the knitwear were exposed, every stitch and seam illuminated by the sun, the quality of the yarns demonstrated in the soft inflection of light as it caught each thread. The stylist served me black coffee in a delicate brown cup that had been crafted on the tiny Greek island. She told me the knit I was wearing reminded her of one her assistant had worn to their first meeting. I didn't know it that day, but the stylist's mother owned and ran a knitwear factory in Reggio Emilia, roughly halfway between Milan and Florence.

Historically, small towns in the north of Italy close to the border attracted knitwear factories and mills because of their proximity to the mountains and the gentle water that flows through them. The rocky terrain was good for grazing sheep, and the water was good for washing and treating wool. By the late nineteenth century, Italy had developed a reputation for producing the finest woolen yarns and fabrics in the world. The industry was built on family-run companies whose owners passed down their knowledge and expertise from generation to generation. For centuries, small-scale firms relied on skilled artisans and high-quality materials until the decades following the Second World War, when global demand for Italian knitwear rapidly increased and the principal manufacturing districts of Biella, Treviso, and Carpi took off. Designers began to experiment with technology that allowed greater freedom in pattern and construction, and machinery that created more refined yarns and increasingly innovative garments. Italian firms fostered a spirit of competition that drove innovation by working with networks of specialist subcontractors who were experts in different stages of the manufacturing process. This period culminated with Italian knitwear businesses securing contracts with prestigious department stores across Europe and the United States, including Bergdorf Goodman and Saks Fifth Avenue. The Italians are still famous for this determined creativity. They are quick to embrace new technology and foster the knowledge and skills required to make beautiful, luxurious knitwear.

Toward the end of my first year with the stylist, as winter approached, she offered me an oversized navy sweater and said, "You'll never be cold in Paris again." It was made from extra-fine Merino wool and had been knitted using a thick rib stitch and a triple yarn. As the days shortened and the air hardened, I would reach for it in the mornings, knowing it would take the edge off my walk to the atelier. Years later, it is still the first thing I put on in winter. It is often the first thing I pack when I am heading to the coast or the countryside. I know I'll want it when the temperature drops in the middle of the night. I know if I am freezing and shivering after a swim in the ocean, pulling it on will calm my heart. I know if I wear it on a dewy morning or in light rain, inside it I'll feel dry and warm. It doesn't retain smells from beside a fire or in front of a stove. In the years I've owned it, it hasn't lost its shape. It is never wrinkled. If it snags, I can make it look almost new by threading the stray yarn back into place. It hasn't pilled since the first time I washed it and ran a cool iron across it. More than once, when I've been wearing it, someone has touched my arm and commented on how soft it is.

All these things are a credit to wool's complex molecular structure. Its warmth comes from a natural crimp that produces air pockets between the fibers; these pockets create a buffer that make it excellent at insulating against heat and cold. It is a hygroscopic fiber, meaning it absorbs moisture in the atmosphere or from the body and prevents the wearer from feeling cold or wet. In a warm environment, the fiber releases this moisture, creating a cooling effect. Its scaly surface can be fashioned into feltlike textures that are windproof. Its structure makes it naturally elastic, harder to tear and wrinkle proof. It generally needs very little laundering; it has a waxy coating that makes it resistant to staining, and its capacity to capture and release moisture means it is also resistant to odors. It is hypo-allergenic, flame retardant, soft on the skin, and breathable, and it is grown by sheep who consume a simple blend of sunshine and grass. We shear it from their backs, clean it, spin it, and twist it into delicate patterns that have graced the runways of New York, Paris, and Milan. Sheep herding does not require prime agricultural land; it does not require plowing, sowing, weeding, or harvesting, and it is less affected by soil and weather conditions than many other crops. Wool evolved alongside humans' need for shelter over millennia. Through the course of history, sheep farming has spread all over the world, and has developed to thrive in increasingly varied temperatures and terrains. The fiber it produces is natural, renewable, and biodegradable, and it is more than likely to have been grown by sheep on a hillside in Australia, where over ninety percent of the world's apparel wool is farmed.

Speaking from his sheep stud, Severn Park in New South Wales, Australian farmer Charles Massy has the considered intonation of a university professor but still manages to pepper our conversation with things like "How the hell did I get on that track?" and, of Patagonia's decision to use New Zealand wool, "Bloody Kiwis." In his bestselling book, *Call of the Reed Warbler*, Massy outlines a regenerative approach to farming that is rooted in restoring soil health and biodiversity. He is a vocal advocate for changing farming practices because he believes industrial agriculture is a key player in destabilizing the climate. He has the deep knowledge of a scholar capable of drawing links across history and the sensibility of someone who has worked the land for more than four decades. Among his collaborators he counts Paul Hawken, Allan Savory, and Patagonia founder Yvon Chouinard.

His farm is located in the Monaro region, in the southeast of the state. Massy describes it as winter country subject to a mongrel climate, tough and dry. The landscape has been emptied by Australia's long droughts, and the red clay of bare soil stretches for miles. Even the air is dusty. A long yellow road divides Massy's property from nearby farms, although if you are familiar with his approach to farming, this is an unnecessary marker. In stark contrast to the dusty paddocks of his neighbors, Massy's land is covered in different species of plants, his paddocks roll with soft gold grasses that have an underbelly of grayish green, the occasional tuft of kangaroo grass reaches higher than the rest of the ground cover, wiry bushes dot the hills, and the horizon is framed by lines of fast-growing native trees. Tall reeds with feathered tips run along the edges of a wide creek whose sparkling water flows clear and fast.

When Massy's grandfather bought Severn Park in 1928, he

encountered a landscape that had been overgrazed by the Europeans who had occupied it since 1860. Much of the grassy woodland native to the area had been destroyed. The Massys were traditional farmers who practiced set stocking, which meant they left their sheep on one paddock for at least half the year. Despite having an interest in holistic thinking and wildlife biology, when Massy took over management of the farm at the age of twenty-two, he continued with his father and grandfather's approach, applying chemicals and mechanical interventions, and pushing the land close to its capacity. Severe droughts in the 1980s and '90s saw him and the farm reach a breaking point; each morning he walked out the door to a drying landscape, a dust bowl that was increasingly bare and inhospitable. He was having grain sent in to feed his sheep, and the farm's debt was mounting. Eventually, he was forced to sell off his farming equipment and half the property. He knew he would have to make significant changes to the way he was running the farm if he was going to retain the rest of his land. He took a holistic course and realized pretty quickly that his practices across key landscape functions – biodiversity, soil, solar, and water – were wrong. He immediately went cold turkey on superphosphates, began planting trees, and watched as the farm began to regenerate.

Today, Massy's work focuses on restoring the land's natural cycles by maximizing biodiversity and soil health. His model is partly based on the work of Allan Savory, who created a revolutionary livestock management system after observing the grazing patterns of wild herds in Africa. The system is called holistic planned grazing, and Massy practices it with his flocks of sheep on Severn Park. He says when land is grazed according to this method, cattle and sheep can play an active role in restoring critical landscape functions.

He tells me to think of a big migratory African herd. The animals roam freely over large areas, hide from predators, chase foliage, and never stay in a single location for long. African herds don't come back to re-graze the grass for six months, so the grass is given a long rest period. Holistic planned grazing mimics this by limiting the time sheep and cattle spend grazing a single paddock to two to three days, which prevents them from eating too much grass and gives the land time to recoup, so the soil benefits from continuous plant cover. The rivets the animals' hooves make in the soil help with water infiltration, and the process has the added benefit of the sheep acting as natural fertilizers by covering the soil in dung and urine. And because the sheep are constantly moved on, they do so without causing eutrophication.

The method presents a significant departure from conventional grazing practices such as set stocking, which allow livestock to stay on the same field continuously. When sheep or cattle are left in the same area for an extended period, they eat the grass and plant life all the way to their roots, which reduces the plants' ability to fix carbon through photosynthesis and causes the roots to die. (For those of us who have forgotten high-school science, photosynthesis is the process of plants turning sunlight into energy by converting water, carbon dioxide, and minerals into oxygen-rich organic compounds that feed the soil.) The lack of a deep and healthy root system damages the soil's capacity to absorb water and exchange nutrients. If water can't infiltrate the ground because of poor-quality soil and plant life, this can lead to erosion and impede a healthy water cycle.

Massy says holistic grazing leaves that photosynthetic or bounce-back capacity there. According to Massy, you can put a lot of carbon into soil and change its color from light sand to dark brown by getting the vegetable matter back into the ground and the soil biology working. Studies support this, proving that healthy plant life increases organic matter in the soil, including carbon and nitrogen.[1] The system is so robust and efficient, Massy says, that once you get your soils and ecosystems working, you can run twenty to thirty percent more sheep. To someone who hasn't spent any time farming, the benefits of Massy's system seem so obvious that it's hard to understand why anyone would still be set stocking. I ask why everyone isn't grazing their sheep this way and Massy's reply is matter-of-fact: the traditional power base doesn't want to change and, understandably, they don't want to be told they've been farming in a way that harms the land. They inherited European agricultural principles and the knowledge that farming is about chemistry – not biology or ecology – from their ancestors. Often, their families have lived and worked the land for generations, navigating droughts and desertification, wildfires and floods, while trying to turn a profit and stay ahead of their debts.

Since further back in time than we can comprehend, more than five hundred different clan groups or nations cared for the continent of Australia. They passed down knowledge of the soil, vegetation, water stores, and landforms and, over eons, developed a deep understanding of Australia's long-term climate cycles and ecosystems. They used intricate cultural practices, spiritual networks, and unique social structures to tend to the land; their rituals were born of The Dreaming (an inadequate English translation) – a religion grounded in the land itself.[2] They lived as part of the natural world; their ancestors had shaped the land, its rivers, mountains, forests, and deserts before returning to it and so the land owned them, raised them, and, in turn, their responsibility was to care for it. Time was circular, and the law prescribed the world be left as it was found.[3]

Europeans invaded Australia in 1788, bringing with them the dominate-and-destroy mantra of the Industrial Revolution. In his book, *Dark Emu*, Indigenous author Bruce Pascoe says the early colonizers described a landscape of rolling grasslands and fertile pastures, kangaroo grass that was so high it concealed the flocks of the first settlers and fields so lush that orchids, lilies, and mosses grew among the grain crops. The colonizers did not recognize that Australia was farmed and harvested, perhaps because the narrative that the land was not cultivated suited their claims of sovereignty, or perhaps because the approach of the Indigenous people was so foreign to the ordered fields of Europe. They quickly imported European agricultural principles, which had a terrible effect on the country's carefully managed ecology, and embarked on unprecedented land clearing, decimating forests of native trees and rendering vast swathes of the country unrecognizable. The scope of the tragedy they inflicted is difficult to comprehend. Alongside the devastation of the landscape, a violent war was waged on the Indigenous people and, within 140 years, Australia's Indigenous population had collapsed to less than ten percent of 1788 levels.[4] According to Massy, the Europeans had failed to fully appreciate "that the land and its Indigenous people were so inextricably bound, that the destruction of one inevitably entailed the destruction of the other."

The sheep that arrived with the first ships ate the verdant pastures of Indigenous Australia right to the ground, destroying the landscape's fertility in just a few seasons.[5] This narrative runs in stark contrast to white Australia's history, which celebrates the pastoral endeavors of pioneers and that the Australian economy "rode on the sheep's back."[6] And for a while it did: through genetic development of the Merino sheep and superfine fibers that are sought after by fashion designers all over the world, Australia became the world's primary producer of apparel wool, a sector with a retail expenditure of $80 billion per year. The industry created wealth and power for the dispossessors, and the landscape was destroyed by farmers and companies that did not understand the ecology of the place they had stolen.

When I ask Massy if it's really okay to be farming sheep in a country so vulnerable to climate change, given how quickly European agriculture destroyed Australia's native grasses, he replies, "Look, I see in books by learned professors that hooved animals are the worst thing to ever come into the Australian environment because it can be more delicate than other continents – which it is, in some respects. But the message from the overgrazing story is that it wasn't their hooves, it was their mouths; it's the eating out of grasses that leads to compaction from hooves."

He emphasizes that regenerative grazing practices can be hugely beneficial – how, along with animal dung and urine, hooves can be constructive tools. He points out that through these systems, a fiber like wool is coming from an animal that is helping regenerate the earth.

The idea that regenerative grazing systems have the capacity to restore carbon to the soil has been proven by Rebecca Burgess in California. Fibershed's Climate Beneficial Wool Program measures soil carbon storage so that wool coming from regenerative grazing landscapes can be verified as climate-beneficial. Her work and studies have shown that if a garment has been made from wool that was grown on a regeneratively grazed sheep and processed in a supply chain powered by renewable energy, the end garment will have a negative CO_2 footprint. One of the studies was from UC Berkeley's Silver Lab and conducted by Dr. Marcia DeLonge, who found that applying compost to rangelands where sheep grazed produced wool with a net carbon benefit.[7]

The excitement in Massy's voice is palpable when he tells me that recently he was looking out across his farm with a botany enthusiast who told him that before whites arrived in 1820, the whole landscape would have been orange. And now, thanks to holistic grazing, swathes of orange kangaroo grass are emerging across his land.

Speaking to me from a yellow room in southwest France, Dr. Helen Crowley also describes seeing habitats in Australia that look like they did two hundred years ago, thanks to regenerative wool production. When we speak, she is the head of "sustainable sourcing innovation and nature initiatives" at Kering, a multinational corporation that owns many luxury brands, including Gucci and Yves Saint Laurent. (She will become a partner at the sustainable investment group Pollination shortly afterward). In her role at Kering, she advises these brands on how to implement best practices in sustainability, with a specific focus on conserving biodiversity when sourcing raw materials.

Dr. Crowley has a PhD in Zoology and, before moving into luxury fashion, worked for the Wildlife Conservation Society in Africa. She speaks with the gentle inflection of international English, her Australian accent softened by years of living and working abroad. Crowley spends a lot of time on farms and in forests and remains in awe of nature's capacity for renewal; it's these values that shape the perspective she brings to luxury fashion. She describes this power for renewal as the thing that regenerative agriculture seeks to harness, evoking similar imagery to Massy (she refers to him as Charles). She believes the farming of natural materials like wool, cotton, linen, and hemp can play a role in healing natural systems. And that we have to move from limiting damage to repairing land if we are ever to meet the targets set by the Intergovernmental Panel on Climate Change (IPCC).

Crowley speaks quickly, naming all the benefits of regenerative agriculture: soil health, plant biodiversity, animal welfare, restored habitats, and water systems. "We're in this really exciting time where we can actually look at agriculture more as a driver of positive outcomes than a driver of just destruction and greenhouse gas emissions," she enthuses, while admitting the metrics are complicated and frustrating because you can't compare an intensive feedlot system of beef production with a healthy grazing system. The latter has the potential to restore natural cycles while it can remove more carbon dioxide from the atmosphere than it's putting into it; the former emits vast amounts of greenhouse gases into the atmosphere and gives nothing back to the soil.

Kering has made a commitment to convert one million hectares of farms and rangelands in its supply chain to regenerative agriculture by 2025 and has an ongoing partnership with the Savory Institute to expand holistic grazing. Alongside several other large fashion companies, Kering has also adopted the Responsible Wool Standard, a voluntary standard for wool suppliers. It covers three areas: animal welfare, land management, and social welfare. The standard is designed to ensure that wool comes from farms with holistic land management practices and from sheep that have been treated responsibly. While the standard doesn't refer explicitly to holistic grazing practices, it specifically prohibits overgrazing and insists soil compaction, erosion, and organic matter be monitored and managed. Farmers must also limit the use of pesticides and fertilizers and improve their land's biodiversity.

The standard was developed by Patagonia in collaboration with several other large fashion companies, the Textile Exchange, and animal welfare NGOs after a video released by the animal rights organization PETA revealed animal cruelty along Patagonia's wool supply chain. Patagonia paused their wool sourcing and pledged to push harder for higher animal welfare standards, stating that they were "currently researching best practices in regenerative farming and [are] committed to enhancing the land management portion of the standard in future versions."

PETA has long campaigned for the industry to boycott wool because of practices they believe harm sheep, like mulesing and shearing. Shearing is otherwise mostly uncontroversial – because sheep don't shed their fleece, they have to be shorn. Otherwise, overgrown wool would get make it harder for them to see, move around and make them incredibly hot. If handled correctly, shearing should not cause the sheep any distress. Mulesing, on the other hand, is incontrovertibly brutal. It is the process of removing excess skin from the hide of a sheep to prevent flystrike. The practice has been outlawed in some countries, but is still prevalent in Australia and the US. Flystrike can be incredibly painful for sheep; it is an affliction where flies lay eggs in the folds of a sheep's skin, which then hatch and burrow into the flesh. Prevention is therefore important to the animals' well-being, but mulesing is not the only way to do this. Charles Massy worked with farmer and scientist Dr. Jim Watts to breed a type of sheep with silky, soft, fine wool that didn't need to be mulesed, called the Soft Rolling Skin Merino. "The fiber and follicle structure prevented flystrike," he tells me, "so we had animal welfare, no chemicals, and all the other sustainable benefits along with a superb fiber." Non-mulesed wool now fetches a premium internationally as design houses seek assurances from suppliers that their products are cruelty-free.

In a previous iteration of Massy's career, he worked with wool mills in Biella in the north of Italy. He recalls with fondness the ingenuity and expertise of the Italians who purchased his fleeces and spun them into some of the most luxurious products in the world. The process of turning a fleece into a finished product is highly involved and requires infrastructure, knowledge, and skill. The first stage is shearing, which is carried out by hand on the farm; the fleece comes off in a single piece, gray and oily. The next stage is cleaning the fleece. The greasy wool arrives at a processing plant, and is cleaned using a technique called scouring, which eliminates dirt, sticks, and other debris. During scouring, the wool is passed through a series of bowls containing water and detergent, and then dried. If debris exceeds five percent of the weight of the wool, it needs to be treated with sulfuric acid in a process known as carbonizing. Once the wool is clean, the bright white of the fibers underneath is shocking. It is soft and delicate and impossibly lovely. The wool fibers then need to be turned into long, loose ropes called slivers. This happens via something called carding – the wool is fed into a machine that has wire-covered rollers separating the fibers to create air pockets and partially align them, creating a long tube of wool. From here, the sliver is gilled, which involves combing the fibers before stretching and straightening them to fit through a very fine comb on the combing machine. To ensure the wool is completely clean, this process is repeated, and the long and short fibers are straightened until the sliver has been turned into a top that looks like a giant spool of thread. The top is spun or roved until its width is reduced by a factor of forty, or to a specified fineness. The yarn must have sufficient twist to bind the fibers together, which will determine its strength and elasticity. For smooth, woven fabrics like those used in traditional tailoring, each step of this process, called worsted processing, has to be observed. For thick, heavyweight knitwear, the wool is spun into yarn after carding, and it is only stretched for a fraction of the time of woven wool before it is twisted. The process is highly technical; creating the kind of delicate knits and suiting fabrics we are used to requires immense knowledge and expertise.

Massy worked with spinners in Biella who were fourteenth or fifteenth generation. He describes how they collaborate with sophisticated engineers and manufacturing companies to advance technology in the industry. Massy tells me that most people don't recognize how good the Italians are at innovation, with the exception of the Chinese, who have invested enormous resources trying to emulate their skills. China currently dominates global textile processing and exports, and buys seventy-six percent of Australia's apparel wool clip, most of which is greasy (meaning unwashed). This is largely because Australia's processing moved overseas in the 1990s, when tariff protections for textiles, clothing, and footwear were significantly reduced, and China was able to undercut prices.

The shift to outsourced production has damaged regional economies all over the world as cheap offshore manufacturing relocated jobs overseas and caused factories to shutter. Rebecca Burgess says globalized, centralized manufacturing encourages industrial agriculture: "When we leave the business of feeding and dressing ourselves to global-scale agribusinesses, we lose touch with the inputs, the impacts, and the land itself." She thinks that bringing back local fiber processing and milling can support healthy landscapes and regional economies.[8] Burgess believes in production processes that happen near the origin of the fiber. If local factories could produce garments with the skill and expertise of Italians, I would be inclined to agree with her. But in her attempts at local processing, she found that locally milled or hand-spun yarns were great for sweaters and accessories but not for an item you would wear as a base layer. The issue was the ability of local mills to spin yarn fine enough for the advanced knitting or weaving machines to produce everyday garments.

High up in the alpine mountains of Biella, surrounded by the terracotta roofs and square yellow houses of rural Italy, are the headquarters of knitwear manufacturer Zegna Baruffa. The company was founded in 1850 and has three processing plants, each specializing in a different part of production. They run on one hundred percent renewable energy and recycle as much as seventy percent of their leftover materials. Their wastewater is carefully managed, and they use clay-based detergents to treat natural fibers. These things are critical in the pursuit of climate-beneficial fibers. A 2020 report from McKinsey & Company and the Global Fashion Agenda called *Fashion on Climate* found that switching to renewable energy sources in raw material production, preparation, and processing could reduce overall greenhouse gas emissions of the industry by thirty-nine percent. But using green energy in these processes is just one component of creating a sustainable garment. If we do not reduce our consumption by buying fewer garments, we have no hope of reversing the devastating impacts of the fashion industry. This is where the other aspect of the Italians' expertise is critical – their knowledge and adeptness at quality, luxury, and style. These things contribute to the way we *feel* in clothes; they are an essential part of our psychological relationship with what we wear, and the Italians have been in pursuit of them, of beauty in the everyday, for centuries. Zegna Baruffa works with sheep farmers in Australia to breed and procure the finest fibers possible; they experiment with twist in the fibers at the spinning mill to create uniquely weighted yarns; they work with universities to engineer finishes that enhance the natural elasticity and wrinkle resistance of the wool, alongside dyeing techniques to produce the most beautiful, even colors.

The knits produced by the Italian stylist came in sage green, bright red, camel, light blue, chocolate brown, and beige. The fibers were so finely spun, every weave was springy and light, even when the knit was thick and warm. Each detail was considered, for function, for form: the shape of a collar, the length of a cuff, the volume in the body. This fascination with detail extended to each moment in the day. The morning began with tiny cups of black coffee. We would hang up our coats and scarves and sit at an enormous round table with wide slats of raw wood and four fat-pillared legs. Sunlight would find its way through windows that ran the whole length of the atelier and onto the old wooden floors. We would have lunch together at a nearby restaurant, wandering the busy streets of the ninth arrondissement, usually wearing something similar – the clothes were so comfortable and chic, it was hard to wear anything else. Often, we would have an aperitif to mark the end of the day. Sometimes there was prosciutto and cheese; occasionally there was pasta; there was always wine. They worked hard. It could take weeks to choose fabrics and colors. Inspiration was so hard to come by and so specific that an entire collection could be born of a single image. Sometimes, tempers would flare, and arguments would erupt in shrieked Italian. Doors were slammed. Silence could reign for days.

Massy tells me about a time he asked the managing director of Ermenegildo Zegna (another Italian mill in the north of Italy) what made their work so superior. "He said, 'I have two children who are eight and ten; they can hop on a school bus and go to Fiorenza and see the galleries of Michelangelo and Leonardo's work. You ask me why? We have an artistic sensibility." There is a pause as Massy considers what he's just relayed to me. "No one else is going to capture that essential ingredient, that tradition and that history. I think it's irreplaceable."

It is fascinating to hear Charles Massy, with his depth of understanding about the Australian landscape, defer to the power of nature's systems and insist that, despite widespread degradation, they can be restored. The implications of Fibershed's data that proves wool can be climate-beneficial are profound. And when Helen Crowley talks emphatically about the opportunity to heal nature through the sourcing of raw materials, she is forecasting an incredible future, a future where beautiful clothes do not cost the earth – they give back to it.

CHAPTER 5

Cut on the Bias

In 1912, Madeleine Vionnet opened her first atelier on the Rue de Rivoli in Paris. Working from this studio opposite the Tuileries, she pioneered a new way of constructing dresses, inspired by the idea that material should move across the body like water. She cut along the diagonal grain of the fabric and discovered that doing so made it more fluid and elastic. The technique would become known as the bias cut.

Vionnet refused to design by sketching; she believed that anyone who worked with a pen did not have a sense for material. Instead, she worked by draping fabric over a small wooden figure that was just thirty inches high and pinning it into place.[1] She perfected her garments by tucking and twisting geometric pieces of fabric into intricate silhouettes that followed the line of the body and flattered feminine curves. She was inspired by the art of ancient Greece and the classical draping depicted in paintings and on statues. Her designs released women from rigid corsets and tailoring. She was fond of saying, "softness is always good."[2]

I have a silk chiffon dress in a mottled pale gray and blue that is cut on the bias. It is wispy and light and feels like nothing against the skin. Its construction is delicate; it plays against the contours of the shoulders, waist, and hips, and manages to be of the body but not at all about it; the fall of the silk alludes to form without revealing it precisely. The silk is ruched into five tiny pleats that are anchored to the upper-right side of an exposed zipper that runs up the back. The fabric sweeps across the shoulder, bust, and high across the neck. It is sleeveless. The silk is draped so precisely that it falls loosely around the body and under the arms but grows taut along the ribs. This is achieved by slightly nipping the fabric to the other side of the zip, tucking and twisting it so it skims the waist without clinging to it. Somehow, despite the chiffon's transparency, the fall of the fabric stops it from being see-through, except for in moments when a flash of the body's silhouette – walking through a well-lit doorway or the flicker of a lamp behind the reach of an arm – reveals the outline of a thigh or a hip. Its architecture is so skillful that its seams are minimal: a horizontal one to add length to the hem and two others to secure the neckline.

The designer who created it studied draping in Paris and perfected Vionnet's art of free-flowing garments that flatter the form of the female body. I worked in one of her stores when I was twenty-two. She sent me to my first Paris Fashion Week to assist her international sales manager – because I was still young enough to fit into sample sizes and eager to please, so I would happily unpack boxes late into the night and haul heavy bags of samples on the Eurostar from London. We were based at the opposite end of Rue de Rivoli to Vionnet's atelier, in a light-filled apartment on the top floor of the oldest square in Paris, Place des Vosges. Each day, we had appointments to show the new designs to buyers and editors from London and New York, St Petersburg and Tokyo, Milan and Los Angeles. The few nights that our jetlag didn't overcome us, we went out for dinner, our high heels slipping on the cobblestones as we made our way to brasseries where we were greeted by French waiters in black waistcoats. We went to parties wearing the samples of the new collection, elegantly cut dresses in bright pinks and reds, beneath shiny black coats. She worked with soft leathers and luxurious knits, with crisp cottons and heavy linens, but my favorite pieces were the silk ones.

I still have a black jumpsuit from one of her earliest collections. It plunges into a deep V at the bust; its straps dive over the shoulders, cross, and fasten to the lower back. The pants fall from the point beneath the ribs, where the chiffon meets in a series of overlapping pleats so that it drapes through the front and around the hips to meet again in pleats in the center of the back. I can pick the fabric up from either side of my hips and draw it wide so the chiffon fans out like wings. When I walk, it flows around my calves, light casting shadows through it, flashing the outline of an ankle here and there as though the silk itself were alive.

The history of silk, a fiber magically drawn from the cocoon of a moth and woven into fabric that is as soft to touch as water, is shrouded in mystery and folklore. Its history is full of tales of princesses, monks, and emperors, and begins with a Chinese legend about the teenage wife of the Yellow Emperor, Xi Ling-Shi. Sometime in 2640 BC, she was in her garden drinking tea beneath a mulberry tree when a cocoon fell into her cup. As she pulled it out, the cocoon dissolved into a long, translucent thread. The teenage empress, inspired by an interest in science and beauty, embarked on an extensive study of the silkworm moth and found that if she fed the worms mulberry leaves, they produced the finest yarns. She invented a version of the reel and loom so she could teach the ladies of her court to weave the long strands into fabric. Over the next thousand years, the silkworm moth became domesticated and evolved into the *Bombyx mori,* and the practice of sericulture – or silk farming – was refined.

The Chinese Imperialists closely guarded the secrets of silk making for 2000 years. The prized material was carried and traded across treacherous routes, precarious mountain terrain, narrow passes, expansive deserts, and dense forests. This established an ancient route traversing Asia, the Middle East, and Europe that would eventually be called the Silk Road. By 140 BC, the secrets of silk making had spread through Tibet to India, and the communities that lived on the Brahmaputra and Ganges rivers began to cultivate mulberry trees so they could rear silkworms. It wasn't until 550 AD that knowledge of the silk-making process reached the Roman Empire. According to another legend, frustrated by the amount of money being spent on silk by his citizens, Byzantine Emperor Justinian I ordered two monks to smuggle silkworm eggs from China to Constantinople in their hollow walking sticks. Four hundred years later, during the second crusade, King Roger of Sicily captured some Greek silk weavers and brought them back to his palace in Palermo to set up a silk-weaving atelier. Eventually, Italy's silk weavers would relocate to the north to establish sericulture on the shores of Lake Como; from there, it spread to the French countryside. Unfortunately, industrialization and the high cost of labor wiped out the practice of raising silkworms in Europe, and the Italian silk makers had to revert to weaving raw silk imported from China – which remains the biggest producer of silk in the world.[3]

In the northeast of China's Sichuan province, on the upper valley of the Yangtze River, lies Nanchong. It is bordered by a misty mountain range, where the sound of soft rainfall is almost constant and, at times, a precursor to the gentle rumbling of thunder. Nestled between the green hills is the central farming site of regenerative silk pioneers Bombyx. Nanchong has a history of sericulture dating back to the earliest times of the Silk Road; here, local farmers can be seen in their fields, tending to rows of bright-green mulberry trees in conical hats and white aprons. Bombyx is working with members of the local community to implement principles of regenerative agriculture in the sericulture supply chain. From the company's inception, Bombyx's silk cultivation and production has been designed to restore the land, raise the incomes of farmers, and allow the company to deliver a product at a reasonable price.

The vice president of Bombyx, Hilmond Hui, sounds like a graduate from an Ivy League university; his accent is American, despite the fact he studied in Canada, and he speaks quickly, with the gentle authority of a millennial. He warns that if silk continues to be farmed using the principles of industrial agriculture, the chemicals in the pesticides and fertilizers will destroy the land. Hui grew up immersed in the world of Chinese garment manufacturing but studied in Toronto before joining his father in the family business. He brings a holistic sensibility to his work and, like many other entrepreneurs of his generation, is wary of big agriculture and its impact on the environment and people along its supply chain. He describes how the machinery used by big corporations to till the soil is releasing stores of carbon into the atmosphere and that over time, as the land degrades, the quantity and quality of the silk will be compromised. He gestures across the fields of small trees and explains that because sericulture is dependent on the growth of mulberry trees, which can be farmed using regenerative principles, silk making can begin with a process that rehabilitates the land and the earth. He calls it aspirational silk.

The fields of mulberry trees are small compared to the flat expanses of crops usually seen on farms. The green trees form striped lines with the chocolate soil and are bordered by rows of taller trees and hedges. The site is over 2,600 hectares and has the feel of a village; there are apartment buildings in the distance, and the houses of the farmers dot the edges of the fields. The landscape is divided into layers, as though each field is a step on the way up or down the sides of the valley. The atmosphere is calm – white fog rises between mountains that overlook the fields, and there is the distinct sense of life being lived on these plots of land. All the techniques used on the farm are designed to respect the land and soil; Hui says their aim is to increase the output of the land and the quality of the silk they're producing by introducing natural ways of putting nutrients back into the soil.

The farmers make their own fertilizers using bean pulp, chard, and silkworm excrement. They collect the weeds from the mulberry fields and mix them with manure to apply to the soil. Even the branches of the mulberry trees, which are cut off to increase ventilation and stave off harmful pests, are collected and returned to the earth. Instead of chemical pesticides, the farmers spray insect pheromones and have installed solar-powered lamps to trap harmful bugs before they descend on the crops. In the winter, they tie rice hay into fat bundles with string and hang them on the mulberry trees, a trap to lure pests that desire the hay over the mulberries and will burrow into the bundles instead of attacking the bushes. To prevent bugs from climbing into the trees, they coat the trunks with limestone ash, and the bugs on the ground are eaten by chicken, geese, and ducks that roam freely among the crops, leaving droppings rich with the nitrogen that is key to soil health. Irrigation comes from rainfall and is aided by the terraced structure of the fields: because each farm is layered, the water flows easily from top to bottom, eliminating the need for water pumps.

The rows of trees are planted at a wide distance so other plants, such as mustard greens, beans, and potatoes, can be grown alongside them. Intercropping and rotational cropping, Hui explains, aid the microbial life of the soil because plants absorb and emit different nutrients, so two species can work in tandem to create micro-ecosystems in the soil. This helps to guard against agricultural illnesses and unstable weather patterns. The introduction of different crops also means the farmers and local community are better off financially because it gives them variable sources of income. "We've increased the income of our farmers by five times," he says. Before they introduced this holistic way of thinking, the farmers were working with three separate planting seasons. After each one, they would wipe the land, till the soil, and all the carbon that had been stored in the last planting season would be released back into the atmosphere. By planting multiples species of crops that are grown and harvested at different times, the farmers can earn money all year round. This has other significant benefits for the community: it means they do not have to travel for work in the off-season so they have easy access to their equipment including raincoats and rainboots and, because they can go home to their families for meals, they report improved physical and mental health.

The growth of the mulberry trees is just one part of the labor-intensive practice of sericulture. The other stage is rearing the silkworms, which is both intricate and sweet. It begins with the mating of adult silkworm moths, which only occurs with the assistance of humans (5000 years of breeding have left the silkworms pretty feeble). This is followed by the incubation of the eggs they produce, which can take up to two weeks. These must be kept at exactly the right temperature until they hatch. There are tales of families in the French countryside vacating entire sections of farmhouses for their silkworms, with the whole family taking turns to maintain the constant, mild temperature they require to survive. Once hatched, they are moved into trays, where the worms are fed mulberry leaves for between twenty and thirty days. In the early stages of their lives, it is easy enough for a farmer to harvest sufficient mulberry leaves to feed them, but this becomes more difficult as they multiply in size and the appetite of the worm grows more voracious – a mature worm is 10,000 times bigger than a larva. Through the network of farms set up by Bombyx, the farmers are able to work collaboratively to harvest the leaves and feed the silkworms until they are ready to cocoon. When they reach maturity, the silkworms are moved to a vertical platform called a mountage. They begin to surround themselves with two long, continuous protein filaments, like saliva. It is secreted from two large glands and solidifies when exposed to the air. A second set of glands secretes a gummy substance that cements the two filaments together. The inner part of the cocoon is made up of the silk fiber – which, incredibly, can be up to 1,200 meters long. The length and fineness of the fiber is what gives silk its luster and light weight. If left to its own devices, a silkworm moth will make a hole in its cocoon to crawl out of when it is ready to emerge, breaking the strand and compromising the feel of the silk. To keep the strand intact, it is common practice to boil the cocoon with the worm inside.

This draws the ire of animal rights activists, but the boiled worms are not wasted; because they are a good source of protein, the communities that raise silkworms fry them and eat them. After thousands of years of domestication, the moths are blind, they can't fly, and their ability to survive beyond the cocoon is very limited, but their lives are valuable in sericulture. If they don't get eaten, they are used to feed fish, or they are returned to the soil. There are communities that raise a type of silk called peace silk. In this process, the moth is allowed to leave the cocoon and break the strands. This silk still has a beautiful feel but is not as versatile or smooth as commercial silk.

Ninety minutes from their mulberry tree plantation in the hills of Nanchong is the Bombyx factory site. When they decided to build it, Hui and his father had two guiding principles: the factory had to be as sustainable as possible, and it had to be close to the homes of factory workers to ensure they had a good quality of life. When many other companies were building factories along the coast, Hui decided to go inland, choosing Yilong county as the site of the factory. As legend has it, this is where the first cocoon fell into the empress's cup of tea. Because they weren't converting an existing facility to be sustainable, Hui says, they decided to "do everything right the first time." They designed the factory to use as much sunlight as possible and covered the roof with solar panels. Hui had 10,000 square meters of solar panels installed, so Bombyx can run on green power from the sun. Because large amounts of water are required to wash, dye, and treat silk, Bombyx is in the process of building its own spinning, weaving, degumming, and dyeing facilities, which will mean ninety percent of its wastewater can be recycled. They use special washing machines that reduce water consumption in garment washing by ninety-five percent, and their silk is dyed and washed with one hundred percent recycled water. Right now, these processes occur at a partner facility that is resource-efficient and uses clean chemistry. The result is silk that is certified organic and carbon-neutral. Hui says they would love to expand the company's network of farms throughout Nanchong: "There's plenty of land for us to continue to convert and change to regenerative organic agriculture."

At the factory, the cocoons are sorted and then boiled to loosen the sericin (the sticky saliva-like substance that holds the filaments together). Then, the cocoon is brushed until the end of the silk filament is found, and several filaments are fed through an eyelet together and carefully reeled out of the cocoon under the watchful eye of a worker on the lookout for breakages or flaws. As these filaments are reeled, they may also be twisted to create a thicker thread. Reeling can be done either by machine or by hand (at Bombyx, they use machinery). When there is enough silk, it is loosely knotted into a skein and degummed, which involves soaking it in hot soapy water to remove any remaining sericin. Silk can be dyed either as yarn or after the fabric has been woven.

According to the Higg Index, traditional silk is the most unsustainable fiber, attracting a worse score than cotton, polyester, and viscose. The data Higg relies on comes from industry and the "best available" life cycle analyses (LCAs), which include large-scale industrial silk manufacturing. Commercial silk production traditionally requires huge amounts of chemicals, energy, and water. Silk farms must be kept at a certain temperature and humidity, which requires heating and cooling systems. Usually, the energy comes from coal-fired power plants. The process of cleaning the silk and removing sericin can require even more water, chemicals, and energy. Some of these silk farms use pesticides and fertilizers on their mulberry trees (although this is less common as the chemicals can be toxic for the worms and the trees usually don't require that much assistance), and some spray disinfectants like formaldehyde or chlorine on their enclosures.[4] Additionally, there are human rights concerns along the supply chains of the silk industries of India and Uzbekistan, where child labor and forced labor have been exposed.[5]

Environmental concerns surrounding silk have driven bio-tech companies to try everything from goat's milk to spiders in their quest to replicate its properties. They have had the most success with spider silk, which is championed by sustainable fashion advocates as a vegan alternative. Spider silk is a genetically engineered fiber, made by extracting spider DNA, identifying the genetic sequences that allow spiders to spin webs and replicating them. The synthesized genes are turned into yeast, fed sugar, and fermented until they become the consistency of molasses. The fake silk protein (made of yeast, water, and sugar) is then extracted and extruded into strands, which are woven into fabric.[6] This science is likely well-intentioned, but the life cycle assessments that pronounce spider silk a green fiber do not take into account the land use impacts of the feedstocks it requires. Sugar is often sourced from corn, sugar beets, or sugarcane that is grown in monocultures using big agriculture's favorite tools: synthetic fertilizers, pesticides, and tilling. To make matters worse, sugarcane fields are often burned after harvest, releasing stores of carbon into the atmosphere.[7]

The visual properties of silk – its luster and lightness – have been successfully emulated by synthetic fibers like polyester and nylon, but their physical performance will never rival silk's. They are derived from common plastics, and their chemical make-up is very different to the protein structure of silk fiber; wearing them is sweaty and sticky in the heat and, because they provide no insulation, very chilly in the cold.

During the Han Dynasty, silk was so valuable it was used as a measure for currency and even now, the price for a unit of raw silk is roughly twenty times that of cotton. The global silk market was worth over US$14 billion in 2020, despite only making up approximately 0.1 percent of the global fiber market.[8] According to the International Sericultural Commission (ISC), an affiliate of the United Nations, silk production has doubled in the last three decades: around 109,000 metric tons of silk were produced in 2020. China and India produce almost all of the world's silk, making sixty-three percent and thirty-three percent, respectively.[9] Interestingly, according to the ISC, the workforce associated with sericulture in India is almost eight times China's; because China's industry is highly mechanized, it employs just one million people to India's 7.9 million. The disparity is mostly due to the processing stage – India's workforce is spread across hundreds of thousands of villages, where they operate handlooms and power looms, and there are almost one million weavers.

Globally, sericulture is considered a powerful tool to alleviate poverty in rural and tribal communities. This is because it can take place on land otherwise unsuitable for crop cultivation; it is labor-intensive (approximately 300,000 households are involved in the production of raw silk); it requires a relatively low investment compared to the returns; and, because the gestation period of the crop is short, it provides a steady income throughout the year, so fewer people have to leave their community to find employment in big cities. Perhaps most significantly, sericulture can be easily integrated into family and community life, and be an important income source for women. This is important, because we know raising women out of poverty is the fastest way to improve the living standards of a community overall. The environmental benefits of sericulture are straightforward – even without the advanced techniques used by Bombyx, planting fields of mulberry trees brings green cover all year round, which benefits the growth of other crops through shade and improved soil health, and the trees easily produce for twenty-five to thirty years with minimal inputs. According to the ISC, sericulture aligns with the UN's millennium development goals to eradicate extreme poverty and hunger, promote gender equality, empower women, and ensure environmental sustainability.

In India, programs run by non-governmental organizations use sericulture to help achieve these development goals. In 2020, the NGO Pradan launched a project to generate a sericulture industry in Jharkhand and West Bengal. Through the program, 3,000 hectares of wasteland will be planted with asan and arjuna trees to host the Tasar silkworm (a different species to the Bombyx that does not rely on mulberry trees). The trees are native to the region and fast growing, so they will be ready for silkworm rearing after three years; the community will be trained in the advanced techniques of sericulture and mobilized into groups for planting and maintaining the forests. An additional arm of the project is dedicated to conservation of another 3,600 hectares of forest. The initiative is expected produce fifty metric tons of raw silk annually, and even though this is less than 0.2 percent of India's total output of silk, the benefits of creating small-scale economies for the people in these communities can be manifold. The project will create 5,656 rural jobs. And, because the wasteland is owned by 4,000 female-run households, by converting it to forests these people are being given natural assets that can generate independent wealth. The project is expected to restore the area's biodiversity and soil health and sequester 1.3 million tons of CO_2 over twenty years. These rural and family-run operations often escape the data collectors of the global marketplace, making stories about small-scale silk makers in far-away places hard to come by.[10]

I can hear birds tweeting in the background as Rebecca Burgess describes sericulture as a dynamic and diverse industry. She tells me about different communities she has witnessed producing silk in beautiful, gentle ways. She describes a community in China where a whole homestead survived on very little, thanks to integrated systems in which everything was used with great efficiency. The homestead had one or two hogs to feed everyone for a whole year. The family members grew mulberry trees to feed the silkworms they were raising and, in the shade of the mulberry trees, they had a vegetable garden where they grew other greens to eat. They harvested wood from dead mulberry trees to build fires to cook with and to keep the house warm. They captured water in buckets from a stream that flowed past the house and used it to degum the silk fibers, then the effluent water was put into the pig pen to create mud for the hogs. In turn, the hogs created fertilizer for the mulberry trees. From the silk, they made things they would wear or sell, and they ate the silkworm moths. The silk was essential to the whole system.

Burgess tells me about a Buddhist silk maker from Chopra, India, who collects golden cocoons from tribes who gather them in the wild after the moths have left. And in Vietnam and Thailand, she says, it's common to raise silkworms at home, to spin and weave the silk and create pieces that can be sold or traded for other items. She describes how these communities make heirloom-quality fibers because the properties of their silk are so special.

Silk is said to be stronger than a comparable filament of steel and more flexible than nylon. Because it will degrade in the body, it can be used for surgical sutures and bone screws. It takes dyes very well and has an inherent affinity with rich colors. It is a protein fiber, so it is fire- and rot-resistant. These characteristics are why people with influence and power wear silk. It is used for kimonos in Japan, wedding saris in India, and for the graves of Sufis in the Muslim world.[11] The Chinese have been using it for burial shrouds for over 2,000 years. Lady Dai, a woman from the Han Dynasty, was found almost two millennium after her death, wrapped in twenty layers of silk, her skin perfectly preserved. Early discoveries of silk are decorated with symbols that suggest the Chinese believed it connected them with the supernatural world. Historians think that knowledge of silk processing led to the discovery of paper. It shimmers. Its propensity for movement and drape is unmatched, making it the fiber that best embodies Madeleine Vionnet's favorite saying: "The dress must not hang on the body but follow its lines. When a woman smiles the dress must smile with her." The singer and actor Jane Birkin was advised by her mother, "When you've got nothing left, all you can do is get into silk underwear and start reading Proust."

The Israeli designer Alber Elbaz, who spent fourteen years at the helm of the French house Lanvin, once described a text message from a friend who was on her way to face her ex-husband in court; the friend said she felt "so protected" by the silk Lanvin dress she was wearing.[12] Given that silk is stronger than silver and gold, why shouldn't it function as armor to protect against the winds of a difficult day?

While he was Lanvin's creative director, Elbaz reinvented the silk dress, using slim lines and artful draping to make silhouettes that could be worn for day or night. His collections explored the nuances of female sexuality without ever putting a woman's body on display. He was not interested in trends and would repeatedly tell the press at his showings, "It's not about what's new, it's about what's good."[13] That mantra reflected his desire to create pieces that could become ties between generations, and so he created with a sense of imagined history. Perhaps this is what gave his clothes the ability to make a woman feel like a better version of herself, as Meryl Streep once claimed of a dress he had designed for her. He wrote in the foreword to a coffee-table book titled *Lanvin* that "the highest compliment a woman can receive is, 'My God, she looks smart!' not that 'she's sexy.'" What does it take to design clothes with the power to make someone look intellectual? Elbaz knew that, in part, this was about how a woman conceived of herself. How she felt swathed in layers of silk that dropped from her shoulder, how she felt in the dress as she moved across a room, sat down to dinner, or walked away. He spent time developing corsets that felt soft, removing the rigidity of the boning and working with seams and fabrics to create a shape that emulated the security of a corset but was also soft against the skin. He did this because he wanted women to be comfortable. His adoration of femininity has been widely documented – he was not scared of its power; rather, he admired it. He was fond of saying that he was not interested in designing the dress that made a man fall in love with the woman who wears it, but rather in designing the dress that a woman wears when she falls in love with herself.

Elbaz understood this fundamental thing about fashion, about clothes. He understood that they could make people dream, make people think. He understood that through clothes we create stories, not just about who we are but also about who we would like to be.

Not only can silk be produced in a climate-positive way, but it is also inherently sustainable, because it is renewable, biodegradable, and strong. In an essay published by the Royal Society, Kate Fletcher says that materials demand in fashion is not solely a function of what people are dressing in, but also how they dress, which occurs at the intersection of garment durability and emotional engagement.[14] But an emotional connection to a garment is not enough to change our dependency on new purchases. The garment must capture something in our imagination. It must make us feel beautiful and comfortable so that we continue to wear it and don't feel the need to buy something to replace it. Of course, these things are ephemeral and nuanced – our understanding of them as concepts may always be just out of reach, and similarly just outside a designer's ability to imbue them into one silk dress. Elbaz passed away from COVID-19 in Paris in 2021. If his creative legacy can teach us anything, perhaps it can be the importance of designing fashion that is so beautiful it can offer something to our deepest selves, to our memories, our happiness, our hearts.

Imagine if these clothes could be created from fabric that has been produced in a way that regenerates the land, and takes care of the farmers and the communities of the people who make it? The current metrics used to measure the carbon footprints of different materials often simplify the dialogue around sustainable fashion to a binary discussion, but sustainability is a holistic concept. It requires a more inclusive calculation to account for supply chains that support the land, the community, and the industry. By farming mulberry trees using regenerative principles, silk production can harness the power of nature to sequester carbon, rehabilitate the soil, restore balance to the community, and improve workers' quality of life. The model Bombyx has created is exciting because it takes care of the local community and landscape, while also being able to produce silk at scale. Hui describes this as "the holy trinity of sustainability – environmental, social, and economic."

As demand for silk grows, the potential for sericulture and silk production to be a force for good might be limitless. It might just be that the beauty of this fabric, which is drawn from a cocoon, glistens like the night sky, and flows like water, can be mirrored in the landscapes and communities where it is produced.

CHAPTER 6

Resort Wear from the Edge of the North Sea

One year, at the end of the summer, I met the Italian stylist, her partner, and assistant at a port in Athens. I had been in Greece for most of August, absorbing the deep blues of the Aegean Sea, riding on the back of my friend's quad bike, and drinking too much Greek wine. The last adventure of the summer was a trip with the stylist to Anafi, the tiny island she visited with her partner every year. On our way there, we were going to shoot the next collection. The island had no airport – to get there we took an overnight ferry that would double as the location of the shoot. It was enormous and old. Its outside was painted in bright blue, green, and yellow; the inside was beige, pink, and chocolate brown. The staff wore black waistcoats and bowties.

The stylist's assistant was also her muse and the model in each campaign. I sat on one of the narrow beds in our cabin and watched her steam each dress, the steam clouding the tiny round window that looked onto the water. Every so often, the stylist and her partner would ask me to be in a shot. It was rare for these photos to make it into the final selection of images because I was uncomfortable in front of the camera and couldn't control my facial expressions well enough to hide it. As the sky was turning dark, the stylist asked her assistant and me to put on matching linen sets. Mine was sage green. Hers was terracotta brown. The loose kaftans had a padded cord that ran around the collar and could be tied at the front of the neck, but we let it fall open. The kaftans' long sleeves fastened with a button. They had deep pockets on either side of the hip. We wore them over straight-leg pants in the same fabric, with a wide elastic waist. They were a heavy linen, weighted and soft; the cuts were generous, so the fabric swamped the body, giving them a luxurious feeling.

The holidays taken every summer were foreign to me when I first moved to Europe. In Australia, our summers coincide with the Christmas holidays, so I understood the longest break to align with the end of the year. But in Europe, the cities empty in July and August. In fashion, you give up expecting to receive prompt replies to emails from the end of June because the entire industry has left their computers for a beach in Spain, Italy, or Greece. Over years, many people cultivate summer wardrobes that can be brought out when they pack for the annual train or plane trip to their holiday destinations. These wardrobes tend to feature fabrics and silhouettes designed for sunshine and balmy nights, for humidity, salt water, and traveling – like linen shirts, pants, and dresses that have been worn again and again over consecutive summers, so much so they are creased and soft from exposure to sun and sea, frayed from having been dragged out of beach bags and shoved back in, between hotel towels and dog-eared novels.

The properties of linen – that it is lightweight, fast drying, and absorbent – mean it has been a staple of resort wear for centuries, likely dating back to the Belle Epoque, when the seaside town of Deauville in France was developed into a holiday destination for wealthy Parisians. The neighboring town of Trouville was a favorite of artists Claude Monet and Eugène Boudin; both painted seaside scenes featuring the bourgeoisie enjoying sunny beaches in beautiful white dresses. The region has long been home to most of the world's flax fields and mills, so it is very likely that, even then, their holiday attire was made of linen.

The drive from Paris to Normandy takes just over two hours. The wailing sirens, blaring horns, and weaving vespas of the city eventually lead to the Boulevard Périphérique, the circular highway that separates the inner suburbs from the outer, and then to Avenue Charles de Gaulle. From there, the route roughly follows the line of the Seine as it makes its way from Paris to the English Channel or *la Manche*, as the French call it. Rows of brick houses give way to sparse forests and small green fields, the sky grows darker and clouds descend as the northern coastline draws closer. Anyone who has walked on the beach in Normandy will recall the strength of the winds, the cold, salty air that rolls off the sea across the wide expanse of gray sand. Every time I've been to Normandy it's rained, even in the middle of summer.

This damp ocean climate and its loamy soils of clay and sand are perfect for farming flax – the raw material of linen. Fields of it grow for miles across expanses of Northern Europe, stretching between farmhouses and old brick windmills, separated by rows of hedges and trees. Over the course of one season, the color of the landscape changes from green to lilac to golden brown as the flax transforms from seedling to flower and then to fiber. Eighty percent of the world's flax is grown in the wide coastal band that stretches along the North Sea from Normandy to Amsterdam.[1] Pressure systems from the Atlantic Ocean move through the area, with sweeping gales of cold wind and heavy rains in the winter. In the summertime, light rain alternates with spells of sunshine. This proximity to the sea is essential to the growth and cultivation of flax fiber. It has been grown in this region for centuries, and knowledge of its production has been passed from generation to generation and results in a type of linen that is considered one of the most beautiful, luxurious textiles in the world.

The process begins in March. As short winter days start to lengthen and the air softens, the farmers prepare to go into the fields. The weather dictates every step of flax farming – a heavy downpour before or after planting can be devastating, for instance – so the farmers closely monitor the seasons. When the temperature is just right, around three or four degrees Celsius, it's time to sow the seeds. The soil is tilled by the seeder's rotor and pressed with a large roller. This creates rows in the soil to catch the flax seeds as they are blown into place. The seeds need to absorb sufficient moisture, so they are sown at a depth of less than an inch to make sure they can successfully germinate. Two weeks after sowing, tiny green seedlings emerge from the earth. After one hundred days, they reach their full height, about three feet.[2]

As mid-summer approaches, bringing with it the warmth of the sun, the flax plants bloom and the rolling fields transform into an endless mirage of pale blue. A flax flower is round and small, with five or six overlapping lilac petals that spring from a pale-green center. They only live a single day, but as each stem comes into bloom at different times, the flowering season lasts weeks. When the flowers die, they turn into tiny spherical seed pods that spatter the landscape, bobbing at the ends of the tall stalks of flax.

When flax is harvested, it is pulled from the soil by a special machine – roots and all, to ensure the fiber is as long as possible, as longer fibers produce the smoothest, finest fabric. The flax plants are then laid down, side by side, in parallel rows. Over the course of the harvest, the fields are transformed from lush expanses of long green stems to flattened paddocks, striped with the gold, green, and brown of the horizontal flax. Flax is a bast fiber – the silky fibers that will eventually become linen grow inside the woody stalk of the plant, bound to this hard exterior by natural pectins. To transform the plant into fiber, the woody exterior needs to be softened, so the flax undergoes a process called retting. For centuries, this was done by tying the pulled flax in bundles and submerging it in the river for weeks, but eventually, this practice was abandoned because the rotting stalks polluted the river, turning it red and gold and emitting a putrid smell. Now the flax is left lying out on the field, where the elements – sea winds, dew, rain, and sunshine – soften the stalks. Through this process, micro-organisms begin to dissolve the pectins and separate the fiber from its core. The soil in the fields also plays a part, so the flax is turned to ensure the retting happens evenly. The retting process can take up to six weeks, but the weather dictates its specific length. The more it rains, the faster the flax is ready, but if the retting period is too long, the flax starts to rot, resulting in weaker fibers. If the period is too short, the fibers are difficult to extract. It has to be precise, so an expert is brought in to determine when the flax is ready. The weather also influences the color of the raw fiber, as though it imbues the flax with the energy of the sky – a season with more sun turns the flax gold, while a season with more rain turns the flax gray.[3]

Just across the Franco–Belgian border, near the river Lys, is the town of Meulebeke, which is home to Libeco, a linen mill with a lineage that dates back to 1858. The Meulebeke area became a capital of linen production in the twelfth century. Flax grows here without irrigation or soil enhancement, and the process results in linen that is so soft and of such high quality that no other region in the world has been able to replicate it. It has earned Libeco a royal warrant from the Belgian king and queen, and a designation known as the Masters of Linen, awarded only to makers that meet the highest standards of craftsmanship and quality. The designation guarantees that the linen was made entirely in Europe, using transparent production processes.

Raymond Libeert is sitting at his desk in front of a busy bookshelf in a well-lit room, describing the history of Libeco, his family's company. He speaks with the considered English of a European, the grammar and intonation slightly reversed, and continually refers to being surrounded by flax fields, giving the impression that right outside his office walls are rolling hills of flax fiber, just about to come into bloom. He is a fifth-generation linen maker. "In the beginning," he tells me, "it was more a trading company because at that time, weaving was done on the farms – the farmer had one loom and they were doing the spinning and everything. We collected the fabrics and brought them to the city." This changed in the early 1900s, when they set up their own production facilities in Meulebeke.

In 2011, before carbon neutrality and zero emissions were in vogue, Libeco attempted to understand the impact their business was having on the environment. They had their emissions measured and began working intensively to reduce them. In 2013, they embarked on a collaboration with a group of farmers determined to grow flax without synthetic fertilizers or pesticides. Libeert says the farmers they work with have also been in the linen industry for generations, and their knowledge of flax has been passed down for centuries. The collaboration between maker and farmer is important to the tradition and heritage of the company and the role the industry plays in building community.

Linum usitatissimum, linen's scientific name, translates to "linen most useful."[4] In addition to clothing, it has been used for bedding, table-cloths, money, sails, and bowstrings. It is valued for its sheen, durability, and absorbency. It is stronger than cotton and dries faster. It has a smooth surface that repels dirt. Water makes it both stronger and smoother, so its luster and tensile strength improve every time it is laundered. It is thought to be the oldest fiber used by humans; there is evidence of linen textiles dating back tens of thousands of years.[5] It was used in ancient cities in Mesopotamia and Egypt, prized by the ruling elite who wore it draped around themselves or fashioned as smocks and tunics to show off their wealth. They believed it symbolized light and purity, so it was also used for burial shrouds. Ancient Egyptian mummies, including the Pharaoh Tutankhamun, have been discovered wrapped in linens. It's believed Phoenician traders brought linen from the Mediterranean to Europe.[6] Throughout the Middle Ages and the Renaissance, linen and wool were the dominant European textiles because they suited the local climate and could be cultivated on the continent. Flax was one of the first crops to be domesticated in the Agricultural Revolution, and it became increasingly critical to Europe's economy throughout the eighteenth and nineteenth centuries.

Now, linen is the only natural textile to be grown and processed on the continent. According to the European Confederation of Flax and Hemp (CELC), the flax plant sequesters carbon – one hectare of flax retains 3.7 tons of carbon every year. Through photosynthesis, all plants sequester carbon as they grow and either convert it into nutrients that feed the soil or store it as biomass in their green leaves or woody stems. Plants that grow quickly excite climate activists because of how much carbon they can absorb and store at speed. The carbon is also permanently bonded in the biomass, so for linen, the carbon absorbed by the flax plant remains in the textiles.

Flax also thrives with minimal intervention and can be grown without fertilizers, herbicides, fungicides, regulators, or irrigation. So even conventional linen farming is relatively sustainable and preserves biodiversity and soil health. Perhaps because of this, organic flax farming makes up only 0.5 percent of total flax acreage in Europe.[7] But as demand for organic products grows, this is beginning to change. Libeco received its organic certification in 2017. Libeert's immense respect for nature is tangible; he says the farmers they work with are extremely strict and have developed their own management practices including crop rotations and cover crops. They often plant hemp, another bast fiber, before planting flax because throughout its growing season, hemp cleans the field by absorbing toxins through its complex root system and leaves the soil primed for flax cultivation.

Libeert describes the flax fields in Flanders and Normandy with great fondness. He says flax is unlike other crops that grow around Northern Europe, because "it's a very natural crop" and wherever it grows, there is an abundance of birds and wildlife. His gentle approach to farming and reverence for ecosystems are echoed in Libeco's commitment to working with the land, the environment, and the community. "Most of the workers at our factory are from the village, and they have a sister or a brother or a grandfather who worked in the mill," he says. By working together, they uphold a lineage of farm stewardship, natural cultivation, and sustainable production established by their ancestors.

Libeert believes it is also essential to limit the carbon emissions from their factories. Solar panels currently generate thirty-five percent of the energy required to run the business, and the rest is derived from the wind. He says proudly that they even recycle the water used in production – "the water we reject is cleaner than the water we get" – and that they have been operating with zero-waste principles since 2016. "In our transformation from the spinning to the end product, even the dust in the weaving, everything is collected and used later as insulation." Libeert describes linen as "really a product from nature" and believes "you can still feel that in the fabric." He tells me that he prefers the natural color of linen, and that for much of their production, they don't use any dyes, instead working with water and sunlight to fade and accentuate flax's innate earthy hues. This mimics an ancestral practice from the sixteenth century, when it was common to lay the linen cloth in the field for up to six months so the sun and the dew could bleach it white. Then, the cloth was washed up to ten times and beaten with hammers to make it supple and shiny before it was spread out in the field to dry.[8]

To turn the woody stalks of flax into this soft and supple fiber, the flax plants go through several more stages, once the retting is complete, to prepare them to be spun and woven. The first step is to collect them from the fields. They are turned into large bales and then driven to the scutchers, where the flax will be beaten to further separate the stalks from the fibers. This process involves using large rollers to break the woody stems from the plants and separate the fiber from the shives. Then the longest, best-quality fibers are selected for spinning. What remains is processed into chipboard or used for animal bedding, paper, or coarser yarns.

The flax is then combed by thousands of pins until only the purest fiber remains. These are gathered into hackled slivers, which are then prepared for spinning. They are combed and lengthened with a drawing frame and mixed with fibers from various fields to obtain yarn of equal color and quality. The resulting fibers—even, smooth, and shiny—are then fed across a spinning machine and lengthened. The speed of this machine determines the weight and count of the yarn. Then it is wound onto a spool or bobbin so it can be woven into fabric. In the weaving mill, the rhythm of the looms can be heard day and night; they operate under the watchful eye of the mill's operators who ensure every inch of the fabric is perfect.

The processes described above are mechanical, which is considered best practice as it is more environmentally friendly, traditional, and produces the most beautiful fabrics. But there are other ways to process flax, including flattening the yarns with pressure to enhance its natural luster, wet spinning, and the use of chemical treatments such as softener. Often, these methods involve large volumes of water and energy for boiling and heating, as well as harmful chemicals. Libeert says that, because they only do mechanical transformation, they are not able to achieve the finest yarns, but they believe the natural look and feel of their linen is what makes it so sought after.

Despite linen's credentials as an environmentally friendly fiber, farming it is not yet doing much for nature. Very little flax is currently produced using regenerative farming practices. Monocropping and bare soil are still prevalent, and so is the use of chemicals. No-till planting needs to be introduced, alongside more biodiversity and ways to minimize the time the soil is exposed in between planting seasons. But there are groups of farmers across America, connected by the work of Rebecca Burgess, who want to rebuild the American flax industry and do so in truly regenerative ways that also provide incomes to rural communities.

In the southern Cascades mountain range in northern California, Sandy Fisher and her husband, Durl Van Alstyne, run a small-scale flax farm where they are testing regenerative agriculture techniques. When we speak, it is the height of a very hot California summer. They have the energy of people who are in constant conversation with the land, speaking over each other and finishing each other's sentences, excited to share the journey they are on and impart what they've learned. They want to become experts on regenerative flax farming in their region so they can distribute information to other people nearby with small parcels of land and eventually establish a local flax industry. It strikes me that they are up against such different challenges than Libeert in Belgium, who inherited generations of knowledge. By contrast, they planted their first crop after reading something called *The Big Book of Flax* and, in the four years since, every harvest has taught them significant lessons.

Fisher worked as a weaver for thirty years and confesses she'd never really considered the origins of her yarns until she received a phone call from an activist who had heard about a fatal factory fire in Bangladesh and wanted to source her clothing locally. The conversation opened Fisher's eyes to the convoluted nature of the fashion industry's supply chains and got her thinking about growing her own materials. She and Van Alstyne purchased flax seeds and found a small plot of land. The first year, they planted in February and harvested in May. Van Alstyne says it was a total catastrophe because of a five-day heat wave that ruined the flax: "The entire crop went to nothing in two weeks."

They forged ahead with more research and decided that, instead of planting it in the summer as farmers did in Northern Europe, they would try to grow flax as a winter crop. "We have a Mediterranean climate here," Van Alstyne says. "The first time we planted it in November and harvested in April, we got excellent quality." Off the back of this success, they decided to lease a 4-acre parcel of land that used to be an almond orchard, and now they plant their flax as early as September or October, to try to maximize the February rainfall. "This year, we're going to plant near the autumnal equinox, so it will germinate and beat the weeds in the springtime," Fisher explains.

They are working with some of the pillars of regenerative agriculture – multi-species cover cropping, no synthetic inputs and minimal organic ones – and tell me this will be the first year they're not tilling because they hadn't been able to rent a no-till planter until now. In the summer, they plant seven different species of cover crops, including buckwheat, sedan grass, Japanese millet, and cow peas, to assist the microbial life of the soil. Instead of synthetic fertilizers, they apply a fungal-dominated compost made using Dr. David Johnson's bioreactor (that has been used to fertilize cotton). Van Alstyne says they built the bioreactor after having breakfast with Dr. Johnson, who works nearby at California State University, and used the compost to inoculate some of the seeds. "The field that we planted with the inoculated seeds did phenomenally well," he tells me. "It was very impressive. We inoculated the flax and the cover crop that we planted at the same time. Some of the sedan grass was up eight feet high; the biomass was absolutely out of this world."

The pair believe that by improving the mycorrhizal life of the soil, they are healing the land. Before they took over the property, the soil was very damaged because of the chemicals that had been applied to the almond trees. "The first year we planted, we noticed that the plants were streaked. One would grow the normal height and then next to it – across a band of four feet – the plants were short, then you'd have tall and then stunted and so on." They work in collaboration with professors from California State University and invited them to carry out some research. They discovered that traditional almond farmers spray their trees with "pre-emergent" herbicides to prevent weeds, in a long stripe about eight feet wide so nothing else will grow. In between the trees, they plant a cover crop about eleven feet wide that they mow down to nothing, so the nuts can be shaken from the tree, swept into the middle, and picked up with a vacuum. Everything has to be perfectly clear for those machines to operate effectively. They believe they are still dealing with the residues of the herbicide used on the orchard for twenty years. "I asked the manufacturers how long it takes to stop damaging or inhibiting the growth of seeds," Van Alstyne tells me, "and he said, 'It's completely gone in nine months.' Well, it had been three years since it had been sprayed and we were still getting these stripes in the crops."

Van Alstyne says that the mycorrhizal fungi has the biggest effect on reversing this soil damage: "Where we've used mycorrhizal fungi, we have noticed that there isn't the impact there was two years ago, so something is going on at the micro scale." Research and testing are an important aspect of the work they are doing on the farm; they document soil and ecosystem changes resulting from regenerative agriculture production methods and have conducted four years of organic matter testing to assess the levels of carbon in the soil. Between the first and second years, there was a jump of 1.7 percent (which is significant as most topsoil has carbon levels of 0.3–4 percent).

Fisher tells me plants used for dying textiles are "her other passion" and describes a hedgerow they planted with over 1,400 plants, all of them California natives. The hedgerow is planted with seventeen varietals, fourteen of them are dye plants, including elderberries and coyote bush. They expect this to provide another revenue stream, through selling the plants, conducting dye workshops, and dying fabrics for people. Because they have restored the ecosystem, the pollinators have also returned, including birds and bees. They also have families of foxes and wild turkeys, and "you can't pull a weed without seeing earthworms."

Van Alstyne says, "It's a magical place. It feels much more whole than when it was an almond orchard."

In addition to dealing with the challenge of adapting flax to the local climate, the pair harvest the crop by hand, walking through the fields and pulling the flax plants from the ground. As this is so labor intensive, it has been difficult for them to harvest everything they grow. And because they don't get the summertime fogs and rains of Northern Europe, they can't ret the flax on the fields, so they have to use one-hundred-gallon tanks. It's taken them several years to learn when the flax is ready, and that it's important to monitor the temperature of the water so that it doesn't cook the flax. They are also trialing other ways to manage the retting process, including artificial dew retting. Another issue they face is processing: without the refined machinery of Northern Europe or China, there is a limit to how much they can process, despite achieving yields per acre comparable to farms in Europe. The pair's next step is to expand into a network of flax farms around the area, to share their knowledge, and join forces to produce enough regional fiber to justify further investment in processing capacity and machinery.

A long drive north from California, following the line of America's west coast, Shannon Welsh and Angela Wartes-Kahl are trying to revive Oregon's fiber flax industry. Together, they founded Fibervolution, an organization dedicated to establishing a network of farmers growing high-quality flax fiber using organic principles alongside regional manufacturing. They are hopeful that, one day, it will be possible to convert the flax into textiles all within the region.

Oregon has a history of flax farming and linen weaving dating back to the early 1900s. At its height, there were 18,000 acres of flax being farmed in Oregon, which required fourteen mills for processing. During the Second World War, linen production peaked, driven by a need for clothing, tents, and rope. When the war ended and Europe's mills became operational again, demand for American textiles dropped. The industry suffered further as synthetic materials grew in popularity and, by the 1960s, all fourteen mills had closed.

"We had this whole system in Oregon, and now there's nothing," Welsh tells me. The closure of linen mills and factories in the 1960s is recent enough that relics of the industry, including knowledge and equipment, are tantalizingly close – but too evasive to grasp. Welsh describes how, after giving a presentation, she was approached by a ninety-three-year-old woman who recognized herself in some of Welsh's historical pictures; she had worked in the mills and the fields. But the woman couldn't remember much about linen manufacturing – a consequence of the sixty-year time lapse between the industry disappearing offshore and Fibervolution's attempts to revive it. Welsh laments that the expertise has not been shared across generations. "As people pass away, they're not passing the knowledge down, and it's getting lost."

In another instance, she received a phone call from a gentleman who told her he had some flax spools he thought might be interesting for her to look at, so she agreed to drive out to his property. She was imagining small-scale hand processing tools but when she arrived, he took her out to a large shed and revealed one of the very last operational linen mills in Oregon. It was still perfectly set up; there were even flax fibers running through the machines. "It was like they turned the lights off and walked away." Sadly, they were working on a deal to buy it when he died.

Another challenge surfaced at the very, very beginning of the fiber farming process, at a point so elemental it's hard to fathom why they persevered. Because there was no flax fiber being grown in Oregon and there hadn't been since the 1960s, Oregon didn't have any flax fiber seeds. So, if they were going to grow flax fiber, they would have to cultivate seeds themselves. They started with a few little handfuls of seed and figured out how to scale up the quantities. They collaborated with a researcher at Oregon State University who helped them, year by year, produce more and more seed. Welsh tells me that last year they produced 19,000 pounds, which is enough to plant about one hundred acres. Finding the acreage to plant it is another piece of the puzzle, as most organic farms in Oregon are fifty acres or smaller, so fitting into their crop rotations can be tricky – and then there is the challenge of harvesting it.

With a glint of humor in her voice, Welsh tells another story about their plans to borrow a piece of equipment from a museum so they wouldn't have to continue pulling the flax by hand. Establishing enough of an industry to build mechanized processing facilities is one of the biggest challenges faced by regional organizations like Fibervolution. They have a lot of interest from local farmers who want to grow flax fiber – so much interest that they can't keep up with it. But they are always careful to explain to farmers that, as it stands, they don't have a way to get the fiber to market. The highly involved nature of linen processing puts significant limits on their capacity. They were raising money to invest in some of the newer equipment they saw on a trip to Europe just before COVID-19 stalled their momentum, so now they're back to trying to get the museum puller running again.

Welsh explains with some regret that it doesn't make sense to ship bales of flax around because "it feels like you're shipping air" and it's too expensive to be worthwhile. Their long-term goal is to build large-scale processing in the region but, as it's not possible to perform all the processes required for linen in a single facility, building the infrastructure for each step along the supply chain is a mammoth task. Determining the scale of the operations is another issue. "We can't have just one little mill in Oregon," Welsh explains. "That's not a supply chain."

Ultimately, they want to establish a linen association for the region so they can share the knowledge they are collecting about organic flax farming with other local farmers and build a consistent supply chain.

They've learned that flax likes to follow cereal crops like corn, and to plant the crops more densely to prevent weeds from coming through. They've learned to plant over winter so they wouldn't have to irrigate and because it improves the quality of the flax. They apply manure to the soil instead of synthetic fertilizers and use minimal tilling. They've learned that flax is a resilient fiber, surviving recent hailstorms and heat-waves better than other crops.

These stories about flax farming, from the edge of *la Manche* to the fields of Oregon, speak to the importance of community in the regenerative agriculture movement. Communities of growers can build relationships with local manufacturers when the infrastructure to do so is in place. When fiber is grown close to communities, the people working the land can feel the benefits of increased biodiversity, rich soil, and healthy ecosystems. Each of these communities describe sensory improvements in their farms, from the sounds of birds to the temperature of the earth, to the animals that appear at the edge of their fields. Carbon sequestration is just one of the rewards; the biggest one is acting as the steward of a landscape brimming with life.

At the end of our time on the Greek island, while we stood at the port waiting for the boat back to Athens, the stylist's partner, the photographer, took more photos of her assistant in the sage green kaftan and pants. It was late at night and the winds coming off the sea were strong, causing the heavy linen to billow around her, to whip against her thighs and hips. She placed her hands in the kaftan's pockets, moved from side to side and swung her arms to show off the garment's silhouette and the fabric's weight. The photographer followed her, the camera flash illuminating the texture of the linen, the soft green fibers shining bright against the black sky. He worked quickly, always without an assistant or lights. He used movement to capture the essence of the thoughtfully cut clothes and the quality of the fabrics. All the linen in this collection was from Libeco, grown between Normandy and Amsterdam and made using winds from the North Sea and energy from the sun. The camera picked up the subtleties in the fabric's weave and the soft inflections created by the mechanical processes that preserved the flax plant's natural beauty in this soft textile, just as Libeert had described.

CHAPTER 7

A Cashmere Coat Is the First Refuge

In 1981, the French designer Anne-Marie Beretta created a long double-breasted coat with dolman sleeves, a wide lapel, and a slightly tapered silhouette. It was called the 101801 and was made from cashmere or wool or a blend of the two. Although it may not sound familiar, when thinking of a woman walking through a wintery New York or Peter Lindbergh's iconic photos of models enveloped in oversized coats on a beach, you undoubtedly imagine a woman wrapped up in exactly this coat, or one modeled in its likeness. The design was fashioned from menswear but softened through the shoulders and made more feminine by the option of cinching the waist. The shape is so iconic that forty years after its inception, Max Mara still sells it exactly as it was designed.

Pointing to the fact that it is often worn while traveling and has to put up with a great deal of bad weather, Beretta believed a coat should be a true companion. Anyone who has worn a coat as beautiful and encasing as her signature one would agree. A coat like that can keep a secret, hide an outfit or a figure, and safeguard it for the wearer or for the party on the other side of the door where it will come off. A deep lapel can protect and shield the face from wind or rain or prying eyes. In the winter, a coat can ensure the bare skin beneath the straps of a cocktail dress won't have to brave the outside world alone. A coat can make pajamas acceptable for the street when it is too early to change before heading out for coffee – and anyhow, the coffee will be drunk in bed.

Beretta knew a coat could transform routine events into something special and provide reassurance during unsettling ones. "An overcoat is the first refuge," she said, and undeniably, an elegant coat with masculine lines, made from something as soft as cashmere, is a wonderful place to retreat to.

Cashmere is harvested from the long, silky coat of the Changthangi or Pashmina goat. The goat is found across Mongolia, China, and Myanmar, along the rocky terrain of the Himalayas, to the place where India and Pakistan's borders meet. The goat has large ears and curved horns and varies in color and build. It has been bred to deal with extreme climates. The coarseness of its outer fleece protects it from fierce rains and dust storms common to the region, while a soft under fleece grows close to the goat's skin, keeping it insulated from the biting cold of the mountains and the desert. This hidden inner layer is the fiber cashmere is made from.

In Mongolia, the second largest producer of cashmere in the world after China, nomadic herders roam between seasonal campsites in the country's vast, communally owned rangelands. They have raised goats at the limits of Mongolia's extreme environment for generations, using traditions dating back 4,000 years and knowledge imparted over centuries. They pay attention to the natural cycles of the land to collect the precious cashmere fibers at exactly the right time, before it gets warm enough that the goat's winter fleece is shed, but not so early that the goat will freeze in what remains of the season. The fibers are collected using a comb with several long metal prongs that are curved at one end and attached to a wooden handle at the other. The coarse outer fleece is left in place.

By contrast, in China, the goats are shorn with electronic shears, clipping off the inner and outer coats at the same time.[1] The Chinese industry is more standardized and much bigger, China is responsible for sixty percent of the world's cashmere, to Mongolia's twenty percent.[2] It is estimated there are over one hundred million cashmere goats in China that are mostly grazed on privately owned farms in fenced pastures. This type of grazing can harm the land, including reducing biodiversity and increasing desertification, problems that have compounded as the global demand for cashmere has risen.[3] It is harmful enough that the Chinese government has put restrictions on cashmere farmer's acreage in a bid to reduce the stripping of grasslands.[4]

Most Chinese cashmere farming happens in Inner Mongolia, an autonomous region of China that makes up nineteen percent of China's total grassland. This is also where most of the world's raw cashmere fibers are processed.[5] According to the United Nations Development Program (UNDP), this makes traceability very difficult as a lack of visibility into the sector means it's not always clear where the raw fiber comes from. There are, however, visible differences between Mongolian and Chinese cashmere. The latter is generally distinguishable by its color and length, since the goats in China have been bred to produce long, white fibers which are more commercial, while the goats in Mongolia produce fibers that are gray, brown and beige.[6] Mongolian cashmere is widely considered the softest, most luxurious cashmere in the world – a status conferred by the length and fineness of each hair, said to be achieved by traversing the most difficult terrain.

From the Altai and Helan mountains to the dunes of the Gobi Desert and Alashan County, where the herder communities live, the weather changes from deep cold to scorching heat, from day to night, and season to season. The intensity of the summer means water and food are scarce. The spring is milder, but its treacherous sandstorms are no less dramatic. The winters are long and dry and stretch on for months. Mongolia has over 110 million hectares of rangeland, and almost all of it is used to graze livestock like cattle, sheep, and goats. The rangelands provide income to a significant portion of the population, the cashmere sector alone contributing five percent to the Mongolian GDP.[7]

Devastatingly, over the last few decades, the health of the rangelands has degraded. The grass is patchy and scarce, the land is dry, and the wildlife is hurting as weather patterns continually change. The region's centuries-old ecological balance is under threat. Based on the 2016 National Rangeland Health data, fifty-eight percent of the sites monitored were degraded or altered, and the most recent report from the UNDP estimates as much as ninety percent of Mongolia is at risk of becoming a desert.[8]

In Mongolia, the causes of desertification are catastrophically interwoven. Climate change has seen the annual mean temperature rise by over two degrees – more than double the global average – and an increase in mining has caused rivers and lakes to dry up. Rainfall has decreased, seasonal weather patterns have shifted, and soil erosion has accelerated. The combination of these factors has pushed Mongolia's weather to further extremes with devastating consequences, but even so, experts consider overgrazing and an increase in the number of goats in Mongolia to be the leading driver of degradation and desertification.

Over the last two decades, the herders have doubled the size of their flocks in response to rising demand for cashmere.[9] The cashmere market is growing faster than the luxury apparel market, with the increase in demand reflecting how fast-fashion brands have embraced the once exclusive fiber, selling it at increasingly affordable prices and increasingly compromised quality.[10] In 2002, Mongolia exported US$45.2 million worth of cashmere; by 2018, that figure had multiplied by almost nine times, to US$390.2 million.[11] In the same year, the global cashmere market was valued at US$2.58 billion. It is predicted to reach US$3.2 billion by 2024.[12]

But this growth has come at a cost, threatening the viability of the whole industry because as the grass disappears, the goats' health suffers and the quality and volume of the fiber they produce are depleted. To make up for this economic loss, the herders have increased the size of their flocks even further, perpetuating a vicious cycle. Encouragingly, the National Rangeland Health Assessment says that seventy-nine percent of Mongolia's degraded rangelands could be saved within ten years if changes to rangeland management are made quickly.

The crisis has seen an influx of philanthropies, non-profits, research groups, and foundations set up in Mongolia. They each have a different primary focus, including establishing market demand for sustainable cashmere, animal welfare, social and economic support for herder communities, policy initiatives, and rangeland management. In acknowledgement of how many groups have come to the table, the Textile Exchange, which usually sets its own standards for responsible fibers, has instead decided to work with the UNDP to bring all the various programs, herders, and leaders together to agree on some parameters around what sustainable or responsible cashmere might look like.

The Swiss Agency for Development and Cooperation's Green Gold Project is one of these groups. It has been working with government ministries and universities to develop better ways to protect rangeland health across Mongolia. Its trials revealed that the rehabilitation of degraded rangelands was both difficult and costly, and that the best method is a return to traditional rotational grazing practices and resting to let them recover naturally. According to Dr. Enkh-Amgalan Tseelei, the coordinator of the project, the research also highlights that from the Gobi Desert to the Mongolian–Manchurian steppe, to the shrubs and mixed forests of the country's northeast, each area has a different ecological capacity to recover and needs to be approached differently. The relatively sparse vegetation of the Gobi rangelands could not be compared to rangelands in steppe or in forest steppe areas, for instance.

The project worked with herders to determine the level of degradation of their rangelands and helped them create a grazing plan to prevent further harm and allow the rangeland time to rest so it could recover.

Rangeland management in Mongolia is complicated because almost eighty percent of the rangeland is owned by the state, so use of it is communal and shared by various herder families and groups. Because of this, figuring out grazing plans that involve adequate rest for the land can get quite political. The herders form unions known as pasture user groups (PUGs), of which there are approximately 1,500 covering 86,000 herder households. The members define the boundaries of their grazing areas and regulate the use of the rangeland with a plan agreed on by the local government. According to Enkh-Amgalan, the Green Gold Project has successfully rehabilitated five million hectares of rangeland by enforcing and monitoring these agreements.[13]

But the Green Gold Project, Textile Exchange, the UNDP, and almost every other group present in Mongolia believe it isn't enough to simply manage the rangelands through rotational grazing and ensuring the grass has adequate time to rest. All of the groups express, in one way or another, that there needs to be a reduction in the number of goats grazing the land.

Allan Savory was born in 1935 in the British colony of Southern Rhodesia, which would eventually become Zimbabwe. He grew up accompanying his father, a civil engineer, on trips into the wilderness. It was on these excursions to waterholes and grasslands that he was first exposed to the idea that the land suffered when there were too many animals grazing on it. After studying botany and zoology at university, he became a research biologist and game warden in what is now Zambia.[14] His professors taught that large animals, such as domestic cattle, could damage the land, unless they were sparsely scattered across it to minimize the impact of their destructive trampling and grazing. When he began his career, working in the wild, he found game parks and grass-land savannas were rapidly deteriorating and concluded, in accordance with the wisdom of the time, that excess animals were the cause. As a young research officer, he recommended the culling of elephants and buffalo, decisions he would later describe as the greatest regrets of his life. Frustratingly, despite reducing the number of animals on the land, it continued to deteriorate. Savory found it painful to watch the coun-try he loved disintegrate into dust and desert and was determined to do whatever he could to save the landscape and its wildlife.

He first began to question whether desertification was caused by too many animals when he saw historical records that showed enormous herds of wild animals roaming the land. In his book *Holistic Manage-ment*, he writes, "The herds vastly outnumbered the cattle and sheep herds that came later, yet for millennia they had enjoyed an abundant environment." The riddle grew more perplexing when he considered the failure of all the sophisticated schemes he had witnessed that aimed to heal the land and prevent overgrazing by limiting livestock numbers. He had seen so many frustrated farmers and ranchers watch on as their efforts came to nothing, and their land continued to desertify.

In the mid-1960s, political tensions in Zimbabwe descended into civil war. Because of his experience on the land dealing with poachers, Savory was given the task of training and commanding a tracker combat unit. Over the next few years, he spent thousands of hours tracking peo-ple across the country. This sharpened his ability to observe and under-stand the wilderness. He realized that where animals were present, the plant life was green and growing. He noticed that while feeding on the plants, the herds had very little impact on them – but when they moved, often to escape predators, they trampled everything. In doing so, they loosened the sealed soil surface, buried seeds, compacted the soil around them, and covered them with mulch – just as any farmer would.

This observation led Savory to the idea that high numbers of herding animals, concentrated and moving as they did in the presence of predators, could support the health of the lands he previously thought they destroyed. The question was how to mimic this using livestock. Drawing on the work of the botanist John Acocks, he realized that livestock needed to be corralled close together, as a herd. But this wasn't enough. He returned to the writings of the French biochemist André Voisin and concluded that the amount of time and how frequently the plants were exposed to grazing animals were crucial to the plants' ability to recover.

His next realization was that animals who bunched closely to ward off predators would defecate and urinate in high concentration, fouling the ground and plants they were feeding on, so they had to keep moving to find fresh grass and plants. The key was understanding that they couldn't return until the dung and urine had disappeared into the ground, which gave the plants ample time to rest. The dung, urine, and trampled plants provided the soil with important nutrients. All these observations combined to help Savory develop a system for managing livestock that mimicked the movement of wild herds so sheep, cattle, and goats could provide the same benefits to plants and soils. It took some more tinkering and a holistic framework to finalize the modern form of Savory's holistic planned grazing method, which is now practiced on more than thirty million acres of grazable land all over the world.

His theory fundamentally challenged conventional thinking about the causes of desertification and overgrazing. Now, after sixty years of investigations that spanned six continents, Savory has found that only two things lead to desertifying grasslands. The first one is fire. The second one is too few grazing animals providing inadequate periodic disturbance while overgrazing plants. Grass that is eaten and trampled without the concentrated impact of a dense herd does not experience the benefits of high-density grazing. Plus, under conventional stocking, the herds return before the grass has time to grow back. When there is no plant life above the ground, the roots die and bare ground is exposed. To healthy landscapes and ecosystems, bare soil is public enemy number one; it is both a symptom and a cause of desertification.

To be healthy, soil needs to be covered with living or dead plants at all times. Covered soil increases organic matter, which helps it absorb and retain water. When there is not enough plant life, rain either runs off the soil surface, leading to erosion and floods, or the rain is absorbed by the soil but evaporates too quickly because there is there is no protection from the heat of the sun, leading to droughts.

Soil health is critical to food production and water cycles, yet each year, the earth loses seventy-five billion tons of soil to erosion, mostly from agricultural land – with disastrous consequences for the fight against global warming. According to Savory, grasslands play a critical role in stabilizing soil health and storing carbon – from dry deciduous forests to savannas to arid and semiarid rangelands.[15]

Chris Kerston has worked for Allan Savory since 2013; in fact, he was one of the Savory Institute's first outside hires. On the phone from his home in California, he laughs easily and his voice is warm. His enthusiasm for the environment and his work is palpable. He begins by telling me about a 2,000-acre farm he ran in the Sacramento Valley before joining the Savory Institute. With fondness, he describes one-hundred-year-old olive groves, heirloom stone fruit and citrus trees, and tells me how they started running livestock in the orchards. The cows handled their mowing, and the chicken and geese were on pest control. They cut their fuel use by eighty-five percent and saw improvements in the sugars and the quality of the produce. He describes Savory as a saint who thinks on a different level.

Kerston was hired not long after Savory did a TED Talk on desertification that went viral. In the eight years since, the talk has been viewed on the TED website and YouTube over thirteen million times. It created a demand for Savory to speak that saw him and Kerston head out on the road. They took trains and planes all over the world to educate people about this revolutionary method of using grazing to heal desertified landscapes. Kerston says, "I've spent a fair amount of time in Zimbabwe with him in his home. He lives in a traditional mud hut on the river; he fishes and hunts; he walks all around his property barefoot." This is something Savory is famous for. According to Kerston, Savory believes you can't "really know a land until you're in contact with it and being barefoot is a way to be in contact with it all the time, to get information from it." Savory is an advocate for relying on your own senses – after all, his first discovery about livestock management came from observations he made with his own eyes. In a way, his deference to what his feet can feel on the ground is an acknowledgement of how technology and city life has caused us to disassociate from a physical experience of the world—walking through a forest, feeling the sun on our skin or the earth beneath our feet.

Savory's philosophy centers around the idea that management must be holistic, and that holistic management is about managing complexity. Like a lot of regenerative farmers, Savory understands, without ego, that nature's vast intricacies may never be wholly understood by humanity. Kerston explains that this complexity is key to the way the institute has defined its metrics for land management. He heads up an arm of the company called Land to Market, a verification program for products like leather, dairy, wool, and cashmere that have been grown using regenerative agriculture on land that has quantifiably improved. The Land to Market seal is awarded based on results called "ecological outcome verifications" that look at soil health and fertility, sequestered carbon, the water-holding capacity of the soil, biodiversity (including plants and wildlife), as well as overall ecosystem function. Rather than prescribing farmers a list of best practices and then awarding them "carbon gold stars" regardless of the outcome, the institute works with farmers to build complex management plans for the specific ecology of their land and region. The idea is to go beyond simply measuring the amount of carbon in the soil, which Kerston says is an expensive and relatively new science. By looking at the whole ecosystem, they get a more nuanced understanding of the carbon model – because "you can't heal ecosystems without putting carbon in the ground."

Even an untrained eye can recognize healthy plants and biodiversity. They are things that change the energy and atmosphere of a landscape (if you are paying attention) and importantly, they are the result of carbon-rich soils. To understand the science of it, he suggests looking at what plants are actually doing when they're photosynthesizing: they pull carbon dioxide out of the atmosphere and mix it with hydrogen and water to make carbohydrates. Carbohydrates are the basis of soil organic matter which trades in carbon compounds. Carbon compounds are the smallest material in the soil, but they retain water, which improves biodiversity; so when you look at the whole ecosystem you can get a robust carbon metric.

Agronomist Daniela Ibarra-Howell was raised in Buenos Aires. She has worked for government ministries and commissions, as an advisor to the United Nations, and as an educator and consultant, all while co-managing her family's 9,000-acre ranch in western Colorado and working closely with Allan Savory, traveling and teaching across many continents. She is one of the Savory Institute's co-founders, and became its CEO in 2011. As we are talking, she is driving to pick up one of her daughters. She places the phone on the dashboard of her car and takes me with her through the hills of the suburbs, and I form a distinct impression of her capacity to multitask.

She describes Mongolia as a landscape that "has been in my heart for a long time because it's so degraded but still quite pristine." She tells me they began their work in Mongolia by engaging groups of herders there through the Adventist Development and Relief Agency (ADRA), which works in collaboration with the Green and Gold Project. "We went to Mongolia and met with the communities, the government, and the ADRA team," she tells me. "We got to a level of understanding of what we could do together." Unfortunately, the pandemic forced them to take the training online and host virtual sessions on the basics of holistic planned grazing. Savory's work in Mongolia is still in the early stages, but Ibarra-Howell shares with me what they have managed to achieve so far.

The system relies on collaboration within the community. She explains: "Whether it's a group of herders in Mongolia, or a family, or a group of landowners or managers, we always need to get to a point where we know why we're doing what we're doing. Do we want to be in this together? What do I need to learn? What are the values? What is the vision? What is the purpose of coming together and trying to do this? And get really, really aligned." In a place like Mongolia, where the rangelands are shared, this is especially important.

The key is to create a holistic grazing plan that establishes "in time and space, what areas need to be grazed, when, why, and how long they need to recover." This phase is a thirteen-step, very specific process that builds an understanding of what forage is available, during both the non-growing and the growing seasons. "If we let plants grow, what is our carrying capacity throughout the growing season there, which is relatively short? How can we honor those recovery periods to allow for more growth, more recovery, more resilience, and all the things that we want to see happening?"

Once the herders have evaluated the available grass and plant life, they can calculate how many animals to run on the land. She says in Mongolia, the problem isn't necessarily overstocking but rather, desertification is the result of herders not giving the land enough time to heal.

She believes that instead of cutting the numbers of goats, they need to organize themselves, and eventually, they'll be able to increase the numbers. Despite the disruptions of COVID-19 and moving the training online, Ibarra-Howell is hopeful. "We have a tentative holistic planned grazing plan that they thought was strong and they could commit to," she tells me. "So next year, we hope to go and begin working in the same footprint." The long-term goal is for the Land to Market program to assume some part of the supply of cashmere, and to work directly with a couple of the corporations and companies that are interested in it. Sourcing this precious luxurious fiber can become a force for good.

Since 1812, from its vine-covered headquarters in Northern Italy, Loro Piana has produced some of finest yarns and fabrics in the world. Throughout the nineteenth century, the company developed a network of textile suppliers before ultimately founding a mill of its own in the Italian village of Quarona. Until 1992, when they produced a jacket for Italy's riding team, Loro Piana was a textiles company, a specialist in rare and luxurious materials. From this point on, the business expanded to exquisitely tailored clothing, from fine cotton shirts to soft cashmere overcoats, from perfectly cut pants to delicate knitwear. The clothes are eye-wateringly expensive, but the family's commitment to quality and craftsmanship is second to none.

In 2005, then-CEO Sergio Loro Piana told *The New York Times*, "I like to talk about permanent fashion ... something that is not thrown away every season. Our items can stay in the closet – and must stay in the closet – of our clients for a very long time."[16] The family's legacy is an obsession with personally seeking out the most beautiful raw materials in the world. They proudly travel to far-flung corners of the earth to source the rarest fibers: Peru for Vicuña, New Zealand and Australia for Merino wool, and China and Mongolia for cashmere.

Loro Piana is one of the only major fashion houses to work closely with the herders who breed the goats, to ensure the native species and ecosystems of Mongolia and Inner Mongolia are protected and that the herders' traditional culture is maintained. They understand that the quality of the fibers they use cannot be separated from the health of the animals and the land they're grown on. It is a relationship they consider fundamental to the core values of their business, something they insisted the luxury conglomerate LVMH maintain when the company was sold to them in 2013.

In 2009, the company developed the Loro Piana Method, a system of selective breeding designed to optimize the quality of cashmere produced across the Alashan Country and Inner Mongolia.[17] It is designed to enhance fiber fineness, maintain a high volume of fibers per animal, and reduce the number of goats to restore the ecological balance between the animals and their habitat. Sergio Loro Piana has been quoted saying that "nature is hard to reinvent" – this sentiment and respect for the inherent qualities of cashmere, its softness and fineness, is at the heart of their projects in Mongolia.

In parts of the rangeland, herders ride on camels through snow, up steep hills, wearing the deep blues and reds of their traditional costumes. In other parts they race on motorbikes across miles and miles of flat landscape that stretches far away into the distance. The magic of cashmere and the enchanting place it is produced demand a process that can support the people, plants, and animals that call the rangelands home. It's not enough to simply mitigate the harm caused by the herders' quest to satiate a global appetite for this fabric. The rate of climate change and the threat it poses to the health of the rangeland demand ambitious goals, more ambitious than mere restoration. If Allan Savory's method, discovered on the wild grasslands and savannas of Zimbabwe, can be effectively applied in Mongolia, the results for herding communities could be incredible. A return to wilderness, to biodiversity, fewer droughts, measured weather patterns, to abundance, to healthier goats with higher yields – and improved quality of life for everyone.

CHAPTER 8

The Endangered Forest

There is a river near my mom's house in Australia that winds through trees and patches of bush. It runs along the backs of houses, diving under roads and behind shops. To find it, you have to know it's there. When I first got back from Paris because the spread of COVID-19 was shutting down airports and cities, I was anxious and unsettled. Every morning, I would drive to the river. I'd park near the bridge and walk right into the forest. I'd disappear among the trees and feel the soft ground beneath my feet. I'd smell the clean air and watch birds circle overhead, soaring through the bending branches of gumtrees. I'd sit on the banks of the river and watch the sky reflected in its surface, the shadows of leaves unsteady and wavering in its flow. I became familiar with the calls of the white cockatoos and learned where the kangaroos liked to lie in the morning sun. The forest had a way of opening my heart and clearing my mind.

Research shows that walking through a forest calms the nervous system, boosts immunity, and improves concentration and memory. This makes sense; what I experienced felt elemental to my body, to my ability to think and breathe. For centuries, forests have been an enduring symbol of another world that can transform those who enter it. In fairy tales, folklore, religion, and mythology, forests are spaces where the rules do not apply, where character is tested and the unknowable looms in the shadows. A space beyond towns and cities, where the uncanny and the unfamiliar reside. A dangerous space where the protagonists of stories come of age by outwitting wolves, rogues, and thieves. Where enchantment is possible because nothing makes sense and absurdity is a virtue. Where the twisted branches and hollow trees may conceal the secrets of the whole world, of your heart.

Forests are widely regarded by ecologists as the most important part of the biosphere because of their powerful role in maintaining landscape functions and stabilizing ecosystems. They protect soil from erosion, regulate the local climate, and purify water supplies. They house eighty percent of the world's amphibians, seventy-five percent of birds, and sixty-eight percent of mammals.[1] More than half the world's vascular plants are found in tropical forests.[2] Forests are integral to the fight against climate change because carbon is stored in the woody biomass of tree trunks and branches, the green leaves of ferns and shrubs, and the mulch and soil that make up the forest floor. While they're growing, forests sequester carbon; according to data from the last two decades, they absorb 7.6 billion metric tons a year.[3]

Some of the gumtrees that line the river in the forest are hundreds of years old. They are towering and wide, the width of their trunks marking the passing of deep time. The memory of these ancient trees and the forests they inhabit runs deeper than most of us can comprehend, so far back in time and space that when they seeded, the lands they are growing on were unrecognizable. But trees of this age and size are becoming increasingly rare as deforestation has swept the globe, clearing between thirty-three and fifty percent of the world's forests. Now, forests make up just thirty-one percent of global land area, and just a third of what's left is considered old-growth or virgin.[4]

Deforestation began thousands of years ago with the invention of agriculture by the ancient Iraqis along the Fertile Crescent.[5] Forests were felled so crops could be planted and livestock grazed. The rain no longer nourished the soil and instead, erosion accelerated, salinity set in, and the drying soils were blown away. The story of ancient Iraq continues to repeat itself as landscapes all over the world suffer after centuries of deforestation and desertification. The forests of Europe were felled in the Middle Ages. In China, overgrazing and land clearing has changed the color of the rivers. Throughout the nineteenth and twentieth centuries, logging and clearing destroyed forests across the Americas, Africa, and Southeast Asia.

In the last thirty years, the rate of deforestation has slowed – between 2015 and 2020, it was estimated at ten million hectares per year, down from sixteen million hectares in the 1990s.[6] But ten million hectares of trees a year is still an enormous loss, especially from a diminishing total. Trees are a significant aid against a warming planet, and cutting them down releases greenhouse gas emissions – either from the carbon stored in the soil or from the biomass held in the trees. When forests are cleared to make land available for farming, it is often done by burning forests to the ground, which releases the carbon stored in the wood back into the atmosphere. Between 2000 and 2010, large-scale farming of soy beans, palm oil, and cattle were responsible for forty percent of tropical deforestation. In other instances, forests are cut down to make things like timber, paper products, biofuels, and textiles. A 2015 report estimated that fifteen billion trees are cut down each year.[7] According to the non-profit Canopy, two hundred million of these are used to produce textiles.[8]

There are lots of different names for the textiles made from the wood pulp of trees, but they are all different types of rayon or viscose (like my black dress). One warm summer evening in 2021, I was at an event hosted by the brand that had designed it. The company's logo had undergone several re-brands since the dress was produced, evidenced by the font on its label. I estimated it was designed in the late 1990s. I approached the company's PR director and explained the story of the dress and how I'd love to know more about where the fabric was sourced. She walked me to the brand's creative director, and together, we retold the story. He paused and said there was no way of knowing from where that viscose was sourced but, given the time frame, it was unlikely they'd be proud of the answer. Viscose in that period was usually sourced with few limitations and little consideration of the ecological consequences. Given the immense beauty of forests, and the trees, plants, animals, and birds they provide homes to, this is a particularly sad truth and one of fashion's most well-disguised secrets.

Rayon is a soft, silky fabric sometimes called viscose, modal, lyocell, or bamboo. It tends to feel denser and more fluid than cotton or linen, depending on how it's been extracted and spun. The best way to understand rayon is to consider it an umbrella term for textiles that are made from cellulose, the building block of most plants. It can be extracted from straw, cotton waste, and other natural materials, but in the case of rayon or viscose, it mostly comes from the wood pulp of trees like pine, eucalypt, or beech.

Despite being described as an eco-friendly fiber because it is made from natural, renewable materials (trees), there is a dark cloud over its eco-friendly credentials because rayon sourcing has been linked to deforestation. Of the 6.5 million metric tons of rayon produced every year, almost half of it comes from ancient and endangered forests, such as the carbon-rich peatlands of Indonesia and the old-growth boreal forests of Canada.[9] Worryingly, production of rayon has approximately doubled in the last three decades; by 2025, the global viscose rayon market is projected to be worth $28 billion.[10] In 2019, rayon made up 6.4 percent of the global fiber market.[11]

The carbon footprint of rayon and viscose is further complicated by the process of turning wood into a textile. Unlike cotton, wool, or silk, which come out of nature smooth, elastic, and ready to be spun, converting a tree into fabric is chemically intensive and highly toxic to both workers and the environment. First, the wood pulp is treated with caustic sodas that have a very high pH. Carbon disulphide is added, which liquifies the cellulose without damaging its molecular structure. This substance is churned and then left to sit, before more caustics are added, turning it into a thick, viscous substance (hence the name). This substance is forced through small nozzles into tanks of sulfuric acid, which causes the carbon disulphide to leave the cellulose mixture so that fine rayon filaments form. These are spun, stretched, and bleached before being woven into fabric. The different names for rayon are assigned depending on the chemicals applied throughout this process, as each creates a different finish.

When rayon was invented at the end of the nineteenth century, it was marketed as artificial silk because of its subtle sheen, softness, and propensity for drape. The First World War disrupted the supply of silk and cotton, so manufacturing of rayon fibers accelerated. It was perfect for the fluid fashions of the 1920s and '30s and, because it was cheap, it thrived during the Great Depression. By the end of the 1930s, rayon was being produced in the United States, Britain, Germany, and Japan. But the dangers of the chemicals used in its manufacturing were poorly understood.

When the Second World War broke out, the Nazis found themselves compromised by supply chain disruptions and decided to reduce their reliance on imported textiles by increasing domestic manufacturing. They turned to rayon factories. The war meant factories were experiencing labor shortages, which the regime dealt with by sending political prisoners to work. One of these prisoners was the French resistance fighter Agnès Humbert, who documented the appalling conditions inside the rayon factories. In her memoir, she described prisoners with overalls that were in tatters, having been eaten away by acid that also left them with wounds anywhere it touched their skin, mostly on their hands and feet. Abuse was rife. Humbert was given little to no training and left to operate machinery for twelve hours a day. She watched as the workers around her suffered spells of blindness, insomnia, and psychosis. Suicide attempts in the factories were so common that bars were placed on second-story windows to prevent workers from jumping out.[12] There is documented evidence throughout the twentieth century linking viscose rayon manufacturing to severe and often lethal illnesses. A 2002 report from the World Health Organization found that exposure to carbon disulphide – the main chemical used in processing viscose rayon – causes a range of neurophysiological effects, including nerve damage and impaired motor skills, increases the risk of fatal heart attack and cardiovascular disease, and can cause blindness.[13]

Humbert worked at the Phrix rayon factory in northwest Germany, but there were others spread across Germany and Austria, and most of them relied on the forced labor of prisoners of war. One of these plants was located in Lenzing, a small Austrian town near Lake Attersee. When it was taken by the Germans in 1938, it was already an important site for pulp and paper production. Its proximity to a coal factory, the Ager River, and the forests of the nearby mountains made it the perfect location for rayon manufacturing and, in 1939, the Nazis built a viscose plant called Zellwolle Lenzing. Not long after, they established a subcamp in the neighboring town of Pettighofen staffed by female prisoners who were forced to labor in the factory in inhumane conditions.

The poisonous nature of the chemicals used in rayon production results in hazardous and toxic waste from the factories. When disposal is not managed responsibly, it pollutes lakes and rivers and poses a serious threat to the health of nearby communities. A 2017 report by the Changing Markets Foundation found visible and highly odorous pollution on production sites in India that belonged to the Aditya Birla

Group – the world's biggest viscose producer. Hazardous waste from factories turned the river water dark red; an independent laboratory test revealed the air had 125 times the level of carbon disulphide recommended by the WHO; the surrounding villages did not have access to safe drinking water; and, in one alarming instance, sixty villagers fell seriously ill and lost the ability to walk. More heartbreaking reports came out of Aditya Birla's plants in Indonesia, with locals reporting illegal discharge of waste by the factories at night or after rainfall and independent testing revealing water samples that showed levels of pollution that did not even comply with "worst-in-class" standards. Similar problems have been reported across China and other parts of India and Indonesia – and the issues are not limited to one company. Inadequately treated wastewater can also severely harm or kill fish and other creatures. This impacts both wildlife and the local communities that are trying to earn a living from fishing or aquaculture.

The Changing Markets Foundation report made several recommendations on how to make viscose rayon production more sustainable, with a specific focus on air pollution, water pollution, disposal of solid waste, energy sources, energy consumption, and workers' health and safety. The foundation suggested implementing closed-loop manufacturing to ensure the waste from the chemicals was recovered and recycled where possible, and that the exhaust air be captured to recover the emissions of carbon disulphide and reuse it. The report concluded that viscose has the potential to be a sustainable fibre if production was improved to ensure closed-loop manufacturing alongside the responsible sourcing of raw materials.

The viscose market is highly concentrated, with just ten companies supplying seventy-five percent of the market.[14] The world's second largest viscose producer is Austria's Lenzing Group, which has spent a great deal of time and energy positioning itself as an eco-friendly company and leader in conversations about sustainable textiles. It has almost single-handedly managed to move the conversation about viscose rayon away from deforestation and toxic chemicals to focus solely on viscose being produced using best practices like sourcing from FSC-certified forests and closed-loop, non-toxic production processes. But the truth about sourcing this fiber and whether or not it is good for the environment, for the earth, is a little more convoluted than champions of viscose would have us believe.

Lenzing's "best practice" includes a commitment to closed-loop manufacturing and promises to contain and recover hazardous chemicals by 2022. Part of this initiative includes clear targets for air and wastewater emissions and innovations for the production processes of specific types of rayon. The company's trademarked modal uses a closed-loop manufacturing process that doesn't put toxins into the environment. It is made using a spin dying process, so the cellulose is dyed before being turned into fibers, resulting in significantly less pollution. By contrast, lyocell, sometimes referred to as tencel, is made using different chemicals that are purported to be less toxic and more biodegradable. Traditional viscose manufacturing can waste up to seventy percent of the tree, but Lenzing has highly efficient systems in place to recover the rest of the materials in a circular economy, so that forty percent of the tree is used for pulp to make viscose or other products, ten percent is captured in chemical form, and the remaining fifty percent is used for bioenergy. The company is considered a leader in sustainable business practices that include decarbonization and manufacturing innovations, but they also consider themselves pioneers in the responsible sourcing of raw materials – which is to say, the maintenance of the forests from which they source the trees that get turned into rayon.

Sustainable sourcing from forests is a complicated business. The Food and Agriculture Organization of the United Nations divides forests into several categories: primary forests, secondary forests, planted forests, and plantations. Primary (or old-growth) forests have undisturbed ecologies and no visible signs of human activity. They are critical to the environment because of their age and density; they have mature canopy trees and complex understories and are the greatest repositories of biodiversity on the planet. These forests should never be touched – even under sustainable management practices. Secondary forests are a sub-category of primary forests – these are regenerating through natural processes after human intervention and, if left undisturbed, may be invaded by primary forest trees and revert to their natural state. Planted forests have been seeded with human intervention. They resemble natural forests and include forests established to restore ecosystems and protect soil and water. They are sometimes referred to as semi-natural forests, and their main use is for production of wood and fiber. The final category is plantation forests, which are intensively managed landscapes mainly composed of one or two tree species, planted with regular spacing and established for the production of wood and fiber.

Lenzing has an interesting history. It still operates out of the Austrian site on the edge of Lake Attersee that was constructed by the Nazis in 1939. After the war, operation of the plant was seen as integral to Austria's economic recovery, and it was reopened with the approval of the Allied forces in 1947–48. Lake Attersee is famous for its crystal-clear water, which extends to the foot of the mountains and reflects the mood of the sky. Conical trees grow right to the water's edge; the air is light and crisp, which is to be expected given the proximity of the lake to the alps. In the mornings, low clouds descend around the tops of the surrounding mountains, slowly lifting as the sun rises and spreads gentle warmth through the forest. Due to its steady winds, Attersee is a draw for sailors who race in competitions in the summer. One competition is named Rosewind, after the easterly wind that crosses the lake from the castle's rose garden, filling the air with the scent of roses. The site in Lenzing is now home to 192 experts conducting research on sustainable fiber innovations and processing methods.

When I speak to Krishna Manda, who co-leads global sustainability at the Lenzing Group, he explains that one of Lenzing's core commitments is to protect ancient and endangered forests. So, they only source wood pulp from semi-natural forests and plantations using the principles of sustainable forest management. The wood and pulp sourced from the northern hemisphere relies on sustainable forest management, while the southern hemisphere relies on plantation forestry. He explains that by encouraging careful stewardship of semi-natural forests, Lenzing can ensure biodiversity is protected and that the forests will be enjoyed by people for generations to come. According to the definition set out by the Ministerial Conference on the Protection of Forests in Europe, sustainable forest management is "the stewardship and use of forests and forest lands in a way, and at a rate, that maintains their biodiversity, productivity, regeneration capacity, vitality and their potential to fulfill, now and in the future, relevant ecological, economic, and social functions at local, national, and global levels, and that does not cause damage to other ecosystems."

In other words, a sustainably managed forest is one where for every tree that is cut down, more are planted, so the forest is constantly being renewed. Trees are carefully measured and accounted for by conservationists or foresters who determine which can be felled based on their size, the health of the forest, and the rate at which it will grow back. This allows forests to be used as a source of income. The Food and Agriculture Organization of the UN estimates that globally, there are eighty-six million green jobs associated with forests, and through sustainable forest management, these industries can be sustained *and* the forest can be protected. Advocates for sustainably managed forestry point out that wood products like timber are better for the environment than non-renewable materials derived from fossil fuels, and that the carbon stocks stay in the wood after harvesting.

According to Manda, people have been harvesting the forests of Europe using the principles of sustainable management for hundreds of years. He says that despite the forests being harvested for different industries, thanks to forest management, the number of trees in the forest is increasing, and the area of the forest is growing along with the amount of wood. In sustainably managed forests, he explains, the trees are rotated on a hundred-year cycle, "so the size of the trees, the age of the trees and the health of the trees are part of the calculation when you harvest them." By taking these things into account, it means "every year the harvest is less than the growth," Manda says. "You might think by cutting trees we are actually emitting carbon, but the sustainable forestry concept ensures that the carbon stock stored in the forest is always the same or growing." He says there are also projects to ensure biodiversity is protected along the supply chain. One of their certifications is only awarded when twenty percent of the productive area is kept for nature, to make sure there are native species, including indigenous flora and fauna. A focus paper produced by Lenzing in March 2021 titled "Wood and Pulp" claims that "sustainably managed semi-natural forests are the most successful way to protect biodiversity."

On its face, it seems counterintuitive that we would look to conserve nature by cutting down trees and keeping a mere twenty percent of the land for biodiversity and native plants (although this number varies depending on the region – in Europe it can be as low as five percent, in the Amazon as high as fifty percent), especially considering how important forests are to carbon sequestration and maintaining ecosystems. I think of the trees I sat under in the forest, and their significance to ecology, to religion, to mythology. To the stories that are told by Indigenous groups, who use trees for ceremonies, for births, for punishment. Although I understand that it's complicated, I can't help but *feel* we should be replanting forests and allowing nature to take over, letting the trees grow old with giant knotty trunks and gnarled branches. Allowing nature to re-wild itself.

I explain this feeling to Rodney Keenan, a professor of forest and ecosystem science at the University of Melbourne, and he tells me that this isn't really how forests work. He says, as a general principle, leaving forests alone and allowing nature to take its course isn't the best option for the future of forest areas. "To maintain a lot of the values you want from a forest – whether it's conservation, carbon stocks, protection from wildfire, managing insects, pests, disease, feral animals, and all the other things that can go on in forests – you need to be actively managing them." He points out that in Australia, the traditional owners of the land managed the forest landscape in a very active way for over 60,000 years. "The removal of that management has had very significant consequences for our forests," Keenan says, "and is partly leading to the kind of large-scale wildfire events that we've had over the last twenty years or so." He impresses upon me the idea that forests are dynamic; they're not static entities. They're changing continuously over different time frames in space. "Old trees don't stay there forever – even within a forest you'll have trees dying and natural regeneration occurring and that happens at different scales depending on the nature of the disturbances that are operating in those forests."

Keenan explains that forest stewardship is about focusing your production in areas that have been disturbed or managed in the past, including areas that have been converted to other land uses like agriculture, so that it is at least partly restorative. The idea is to return trees to previously cleared land and do it in a way that allows for both production of timber and other materials while the landscape is being maintained for conservation outcomes. He says that the forests in Europe were mostly naturally regenerated following large-scale disturbances and that a lot of modern forestry in Europe is about replanting those areas and re-establishing trees. As a result, there's a whole range of forest management in Europe, including different philosophies and efforts to move away from large-scale industrial harvesting toward close-to-nature forestry or constant-cover forestry.

The different approaches are embodied in countless government and industry-based organizations that are rolling out plans to protect and restore forests all over the world. Their strategies include standards and certifications, anti-logging laws, the protection of indigenous lands, guidelines for sustainable timber and agricultural practices, and programs enabling wealthy nations and corporations to pay countries for maintaining tropical forests.

More than ninety-nine percent of the wood and dissolving pulp used by Lenzing is from semi-natural forests or plantations that have received a sustainable certification from either the Forest Stewardship Council (FSC) or the Programme for the Endorsement of Forest Certification (PEFC). Both are broadly accepted international programs to apply technical standards of forest management in different countries. FSC was founded in 1993 and sets standards for responsible forest management and chains of custody to guarantee where the trees were sourced. PEFC was founded in 1999 and is a global alliance of national forest certification systems and the largest forest certification system worldwide. In the last two decades, the forest area certified as meeting FSC or PEFC standards has increased from roughly one percent to ten percent of all forests.

Lenzing often points to the work it does with the non-profit Canopy to highlight their eco-friendly credentials. Canopy works to secure large-scale forest conservation and transform unsustainable forest product supply chains by working directly with the industry. They have partnered with designers like Stella McCartney and Eileen Fisher and, at the end of 2020, they conducted an independent audit of Lenzing's pulp sourcing. This audit confirmed Lenzing is at "low risk of sourcing wood from ancient or endangered forests or other controversial sources." But despite Lenzing and other fashion houses promoting their connection to Canopy to prove the sustainability of their viscose and rayon sourcing, my conversation with Canopy revealed a more nuanced position.

Amanda Carr is the senior lead on the CanopyStyle campaign. Via email, Carr tells me that "CanopyStyle is dedicated to systemic change in the sourcing of pulp for textiles across this particular supply chain, including viscose, rayon, modal, lyocell, acetate, and all the trademarked brands in between." Their priority is to ensure no viscose is sourced from ancient and endangered forests, and she says the next step is to replace fiber from forests with fiber from a more sustainable source. Their preference is for next-generation solutions like using old clothing to make new pulp, or growing fiber from yeast or food waste. "It's important to note that conserving forests is thought to be able to provide about thirty percent of the solution to the climate crisis," she says – a figure reiterated by United Nations Environment Programme.[15]

She explains why it's so complicated to classify different forests to determine what sustainable sourcing looks like. While sourcing wood products and pulp from plantations may be cited as a sustainable alternative by companies like Lenzing, she says, "all too often, plantations have come at a cost of recent deforestation in places like Indonesia's rainforests, for example, so a blanket statement that plantations are the most sustainable isn't accurate." Furthermore, some "secondary forests are very old and, if left unharvested, have the potential to begin to provide the kind of eco-services (storing carbon, filtering water, regulating rainfall) that ancient forests do." When she writes that "we don't see easy, cut-and-dry answers to these types of questions," I feel vindicated after months of complicated reading and mind-bending conversations with experts. Canopy's position with regard to viscose rayon seems to be: ensure there is no sourcing from ancient or endangered forests, or from plantations that have caused deforestation and destroyed the habitat of any endangered species, and then transition all viscose sourcing away from forests, secondary or otherwise, toward recycled cellulose options.

This goal is at odds with Lenzing's strategy, which continues to source from plantations and forests – albeit those with FSC certifications. But of course, the reality of the supply chain means it is not quite so simple.

In order to protect ancient and endangered forests, Carr says, sometimes trade-offs need to be made so fiber supply can be satisfied – "for example, more intensive plantation management on degraded lands to concentrate fiber production." Some of this is mapped out in Canopy's *Survival* plan, which includes a hierarchy of strategies: first conserve and reduce; then maximize the use of the lowest footprint fibers (recycled and next generation); then, where virgin inputs are still required, explore potentially fast-growing, on-purpose crops (like bast fibers) that are grown under specific standards for managing environmental impacts; and then, trees from plantations on degraded lands may have a role as well. She describes how nuanced it is to develop priorities for restoration and protection in different landscapes. Sometimes, it involves restoring plantations back to secondary and then primary forests, in order to return forest ecosystems to an appropriate level of conservation.

At the same time, she flags that "it feels like a human-centric notion to assume we could possibly do better for our plant, our biodiversity, and our climate by managing a complex forest ecosystem for resource extraction or even tree growth ... They simply need to be left standing and providing for the cultures and communities that have safeguarded them for millennia to have the biggest benefit." She tells me that, in some circumstances, there is not an option for sustainably managed forestry because some forest ecosystems or landscapes are irreplaceable.

Still, she concedes the forest certifications, like the ones Lenzing uses, are "a good tool," and that FSC certification offers the highest level of confidence. But they are constrained by scale because certification is applied from a local viewpoint, without considering regional or global needs. Governance is another constraint; regulations must be developed in alignment with indigenous and traditional governance to determine what should be conserved and what should be extracted across entire ecosystems. "This is not the kind of planning that voluntary certification applied by individual corporations accomplishes."

Interestingly, Carr is adamant that "trees left standing sequester more carbon over time." This makes sense, but it does contradict experts such as Manda, who insist new or growing trees sequester more carbon than those left standing. This bothered me – all I could think of was how the new forests I had visited in Europe compared to the depth and height of the Australian bush. The new forests felt sad and sparse, while in Australia, forests feel mysterious and alive. Carr cites studies that suggest approximately fifty percent of the carbon is left in a clear cut or harvest block after trees have been cut for forest products – in the soils, root systems, broken branches, leaves, and so on. Had the trees been left in the forest, this carbon would have remained sequestered in a standing forest ecosystem, but instead, it quickly biodegrades in one or two years and releases carbon into the atmosphere.

In its *Survival* action plan, Canopy advocates for moving away from forests as a source of the raw material for viscose and rayon. The plan outlines a strategy to reduce the amount of forest fiber going into the manufacturing of pulp for paper, packaging, and viscose fabrics by switching to alternative materials like agricultural waste and recycled cellulose from textile waste. According to Textile Exchange, the market share of "recycled" cellulose fibers is very small, but a lot of ongoing research and development means it is expected to increase significantly in the coming years. Recent technological advancements have made it possible to convert some textile waste into new materials. Any plant-based material can potentially serve as a source of cellulose and be dissolved to make fibers, so theoretically all natural fabrics like cotton, linen, and silk could be regenerated into viscose rayon. Canopy says this creates an opportunity to recycle a fraction of the twenty million tons of cotton fabric waste and the six million tons of viscose fabric waste generated every year back into viscose pulp. The process is much more efficient than converting trees. "On average, it takes 2.5–3 tons of trees to create 1 ton of viscose pulp, but it takes only about 1 ton of recycled cotton or rayon to make 1 ton of viscose pulp.'[16] There are other things to consider in the equation, like the source of the energy required. Lenzing uses the remaining wood pulp to create bioenergy and other products, so the process is zero-waste, but their best practice represents just one part of the supply chain and is not widely adopted by other companies.

Carr confirms Canopy's position that, rather than sourcing cellulose from trees, "all new investments and infrastructure should be focused on using next-generation fibers – targeting textile waste and circularity are key priorities." She says a wonderful reality of working in this forest-based fabric supply chain is the opportunity to steer investments toward solutions and away from problems. "It is like we are standing on a cliff edge, and we have an opportunity to build a fence at the top versus a hospital at the bottom."

It's important to acknowledge that Lenzing is part of this mission. They have done significant research on alternative, non-wood cellulose sources and concluded that textile waste can be a valuable raw material for the production of viscose rayon. And they have developed fabrics made from pre-consumer cotton scraps and post-consumer garments combined with wood pulp. Carr says that even though CanopyStyle has confirmed Lenzing has a low risk of sourcing from the world's ancient and endangered forests, "at the end of the day, the best thing to do if you had to source viscose from Lenzing would be to buy their recycled line, where they are blending thirty percent textile waste into the mix of their Refibra product line."

Ultimately, sourcing viscose rayon from forests does not have the same potential for regeneration as the farming of other natural fibers. But since the science used to take wood pulp and turn it into a fabric can be applied to transform textile waste into an input material, there is still potential for viscose rayon production to become a force for good. Textile waste is an insurmountable problem for the fashion industry because of the volume of clothes being discarded and, much like rubbish made of plastic, this waste isn't going away. Synthetic fibers won't biodegrade, and natural fibers have to be disposed of in the right circumstances (like compost), so we need innovative solutions to the problem created by the tons of textile waste sent to landfill every second. That makes the notion that we can turn old textiles into new ones that are superior to synthetics extremely interesting. Since viscose rayon is made of cellulose, it is better on the body and for the environment than synthetics; it breathes against the skin and does not have a complicated relationship with oil or sweat, which makes it nicer to wear, and it doesn't shed plastic microfibers into waterways every time it's washed.

This means that, despite viscose rayon's dark and complex history, which in many ways extends into the present, it could have a hopeful future. If we can eliminate trees and forests from its sourcing, transition to sourcing from textile waste and bast fibers and further innovate production to be closed-loop and non-toxic, viscose rayon could truly earn the eco-friendly reputation it has already been given – which is very good news. The fashion industry faces an extremely complex set of problems that touch every single part of the supply chain. To solve these problems and move beyond sustainability, fashion needs to embrace many and varied innovative solutions. We really are just at the beginning of this journey, staring down a long road to get to a place where the clothes we create are doing more good than harm.

CHAPTER 9

Patagonia and the Ingenuity of Hemp

A small, beat-up car drives along a wide dirt road toward a snow-capped mountain range on the border between Argentina and Chile. In the distance, the mountain Fitz Roy, or Cerro Chaltén, is craggy and peaked; the road stretches long and straight across the flat desert. The old car has piles of gear strapped to its roof, and through the back window, you can see the crowded heads of its passengers.

This particular photo was taken by Barbara Rowell for the outdoor clothing brand Patagonia in 1985. It captures the essence of the brand's founder Yvon Chouinard, who wasn't in the car that day but has spent the last sixty-something years trekking into far-flung, hard-to-reach places. In his book *Let My People Go Surfing,* Chouinard describes driving to Wyoming at the age of sixteen, hiking the biggest mountain and spending the rest of the summer learning to climb in the Tetons. He spent his school holidays surfing off the coast of Mexico. Eventually, the young Chouinard befriended other climbers, and together, they journeyed to Yosemite to tackle the park's biggest walls. Over several decades, the trips would take him from Canada to the Alps, from Ventura to South America, from volcanoes in Chile to the wilderness of Patagonia – the place that would eventually become the name of his outdoor clothing business, which would one day become a global empire.

From the beginning, Chouinard set out to make things that allowed people to live close to nature. He had spent much of his life living and working out of the back of his car, sleeping outside, beneath boulders or the low-hanging branches of alpine fir trees. He described his kind as "like the wild species living on the edge of an ecosystem – adaptable, resilient and tough."

He started making his own climbing hardware in 1957. Frustrated with the only available European pitons that had to be left in the rock face, he felt you should leave no trace when you climbed mountains or visited the wilderness and so created stiffer, stronger pitons that could be removed and used over and over again. He called them Lost Arrows; it took half an hour to forge one and he sold them for $1.50 each. Eventually, he invested in more equipment so he could expand and started making carabiners. Since most of his equipment was portable, he would load up his car and travel up and down the California coast, from Big Sur to San Diego, surfing and forging pitons in turns.

About a decade later, he expanded the range of climbing equipment to include clothes after coming across an old mill in England that dated back to the Industrial Revolution. The mill manufactured the fabric for the "original" workman pants, which were made of corduroy. Chouinard recognized that cord would be good for climbing and used it to make double-seated shorts that were a big success among his fellow mountaineers. A few years later, he started importing brightly colored rugby shirts in blue, red, and yellow from Scotland. By 1972, the line had expanded to backpacks, gloves, and hats. Soon, they were making more and more clothes – wool Chamonix guide sweaters, classic Mediterranean sailor shirts, canvas pants and shorts, and technical rainwear.

An early Patagonia catalogue promised to inspire "romantic visions of glaciers tumbling into fjords; jagged, windswept peaks; gauchos, and condors." The accompanying images were of bright white snow against blue skies, with a man or woman wearing a fire-engine-red jacket navigating the terrain. In other shots, bare-chested climbers scaled rugged rock walls in beige shorts. There were breathtaking photos of friends sleeping in hammocks hoisted between cliffs, of surfers riding clear blue waves in shiny wetsuits. They introduced more shades and more options. T-shirts, shirts, and shorts in cobalt, teal, mango, seafoam, and iced mocha. The inhabitants of these catalogues, of Chouinard's world, lived in technicolor.

From the mid-1980s to 1990, sales grew from $20 million to $100 million. The rapid growth was unsettling for Chouinard, who felt that the pressure to mass produce would compromise their basic design principle: to make the best product. He was also growing increasingly aware of the deterioration of the natural world. When he returned to climb or surf or fish in places he knew well, like Nepal, Africa, and Polynesia, the environmental and social devastation of the landscapes haunted him. Grasslands were disappearing, glaciers were melting, forests were being cleared, wild animals were fewer, and concrete development was spreading. He learned from books and newspapers that topsoil and groundwater were disappearing, plants and animals were endangered, the people in the Arctic couldn't eat local animals and fish because of toxics from the industrialized West.

Patagonia's environmentalism began with a local surf break that was under threat from the City of Ventura's plan to channel and develop the mouth of a nearby river. The young activist organizing the fight to stop them was given a desk at Patagonia headquarters and access to the company's resources. Soon, Chouinard's concerns for the future of the climate and the natural world infiltrated his business, causing him to take a hard look at how the company operated and the environmental impact of the products it was making. The company created a set of philosophies that would guide every decision made within the business, beginning with: "All decisions of the company are made within the context of the environmental crisis. We must strive to do no harm. "

The business's first environmental report was released in 1994. By the spring of 1996, the only cotton they used was organic and other material innovations (including recycled polyester) followed. Since then, the business has given the equivalent of $116 million to environmental causes, in part through a commitment to donate one percent of their annual revenue primarily to grassroots environmental non-profits. They have pledged to be carbon-neutral by 2025 and have invested in recycling and repair initiatives. But, their most interesting environmental work is the close relationships they have fostered with farmers of raw materials. Through these collaborations, they have created guiding principles and invested in research and education so the natural fibers they source could be farmed using regenerative organic principles. In 2018, Patagonia and a coalition of like-minded farmers, ranchers, brands, non-profits, and other organizations created the Regenerative Organic Certification, an all-encompassing regenerative standard that moves beyond existing organic principles in agriculture and adds requirements for soil health, animal welfare, and social fairness. The pilot launched with twenty farms around the world growing grains, fruits, and cotton and will eventually expand to other natural fibers like wool, linen, and hemp.

Hemp is often cited by sustainable fashion advocates as a fiber of the future because it can regenerate the land where it's planted. In the right region, it grows with minimal fertilizers and pesticides and without irrigation. It also has great potential for carbon sequestration and soil health. But, it makes up a very small percentage of the fiber market, and its capacity to be used as a mainstream textile remains relatively untested. This makes it something of an enigma, which is intensified by its complicated history. For a long time, because of its close relationship to marijuana (they are both part of the cannabis family), growing hemp was prohibited across much of the Western world and was only removed from the UN's Schedule IV Prohibition in 2020.

Chouinard first expressed an interest in hemp in 1993, when the company's environmental philosophies were being formed. After seeing old Japanese hemp kimonos that were still beautiful after years of wear, he told his team he wanted this longevity in Patagonia's sportswear line. Hemp cultivation was banned in the United States at the time, and sourcing the fiber proved difficult. Eventually, research revealed that China was the place to find it and Jill Dumain, then the company's director of fabric development, traveled to China in search of a hemp supplier.

In *Let My People Go Surfing*, Dumain describes coming to the end of a long, winding road that led to a remote village in the mountains of China's Shaanxi Province and discovering the farms where Patagonia's hemp would be grown. The crops were rain-fed. Chickens and cattle roamed the land, providing fertilizer. They didn't use herbicides or insecticides. Bundles of hemp stood in the fields, drying until the stalks were ready to be submerged in the river for retting.[1] Almost thirty years later, Patagonia is still working with these hemp farmers in Shaanxi Province.

Hemp is a bast fiber, like flax, except it grows up to thirteen feet tall, so it completely dwarfs any farmers who walk beside it. Hemp plants are long and straight, with hollow woody stalks. Industrial hemp is naturally resistant to bugs, so it requires no insecticides, its rapid canopy growth suppresses weeds, so it doesn't require herbicides. It is so robust that it can resist frost and can grow in many kinds of soils. It actively improves soil structure because its long roots can tap into sub-soil nutrients other plants can't access. A four-year trial by the Rodale Institute found that hemp even mines and accumulates heavy metals, making it a viable bioremediation crop.[2]

All of this sounds pretty incredible, but what has climate activists and sustainable designers most excited is hemp's potential to sequester carbon. While it's growing, like all plants, hemp absorbs carbon and stores it as biomass – but because hemp grows so fast, so tall, and in such high density, it is considered one of the most efficient commercial crops for carbon sequestration. The CO_2 is permanently bonded within the fiber and whatever material it is turned into. Darshil Shah, a researcher at Cambridge University, says one hectare of industrial hemp can absorb 10–15 tonnes of CO_2, which is twice as much as a forest. Hemp reaches its full height in just 100 days, and because it's possible to grow two crops per year, that rate of carbon absorption can be doubled.

Hemp can be cultivated for seed and oil or fiber. Hemp seed and the oil derived from it are considered superfoods that are extremely high in protein, minerals like potassium and magnesium as well as essential ammino acids. Hemp's other applications range from bioplastics to superfoods, paper products, building materials and biofuel.

Hemp cultivation dates back at least 12,000 years. It is considered one of the earliest domesticated crops, and because it is extremely versatile, it quickly spread across the globe. Historical records suggest the Chinese cultivated it for fiber, seeds, and oil 4,500 years ago. In the early Christian era, hemp spread throughout the Mediterranean; by the Middle Ages it had reached the rest of Europe. In the 1500s, it was planted in Chile, and one hundred years later in North America.[3] Hemp paper is said to have been used for important writing, such as early bibles and laws. As the European powers battled for nautical supremacy in the seventeenth and eighteenth centuries, hemp was vital as it made excellent ropes, sails, rigging, ladders, lanyards, and fishing lines. It was a widespread but relatively ordinary crop for thousands of years – until the twentieth century, when its popularity began to decline with the rise of petrochemicals, synthetic fibers, and cotton. This slowdown culminated in a strange twist when, in 1937, the *Marihuana Tax Act* was passed in the United States; suddenly, growing hemp was illegal.

The Act was part of a crackdown on drugs, and was reinforced by the *Controlled Substances Act* in the 1970s. Hemp's inclusion is thought to have been because of confusion on behalf of lawmakers couldn't distinguish it from its sister plant, marijuana. The key distinction between the two plants is that hemp does not have psychoactive properties. The chemical in marijuana that gets people high is called tetrahydrocannabinol (THC), and while it is found in hemp, it's at tiny percentages (the legal requirement is between 0.3–1 percent) compared to marijuana, which has THC levels of about twenty percent.

There are also suggestions that hemp's inclusion was the result of lobbying from powerful bodies who wanted to capitalize on its prohibition. In her book *Fibershed*, Rebecca Burgess points out that hemp was rarely grown in association with marijuana because it easily cross-pollinated and reduced the latter's psychoactive impacts – which isn't something marijuana growers want. "And yet," she writes, "this horticultural knowledge was somehow left out of our drug laws." Once the laws were passed, hemp was no longer regulated by the agricultural sector but by the federal Drug Enforcement Agency (DEA). This change in classification spread around the globe, and hemp farming was banned in most Western countries. Despite having cultivated it for thousands of years, China also banned it in 1985 when joining the UN Convention on Psychotropic Substances. Finally, in the 1990s, attitudes toward hemp and its classification as an illicit substance were reassessed as concern for the environment and consumption of natural resources led industry and government to consider alternative fuel sources. In 1992, France, The Netherlands, England, Spain, and Germany legalized the commercial cultivation of low-THC hemp, followed by Canada in 1994 and China in 2010.[4] Commercial cultivation of hemp remained illegal in the United States until the 2018 Farm Bill was passed.

Sitting in his office on Funky Butte Ranch in New Mexico, Doug Fine is wearing a straw hat, and all around him there are tiny scraps of paper hanging from the roof and the walls of the small room. He says most of them are his kid's artwork, except for one larger piece on the wall behind him. He explains proudly that it is a replica of the draft of the Declaration of Independence, which is said to have been written on hemp paper. Fine swigs green liquid from a large glass jar, he tells me it's matcha tea with a little goat's milk (from the ranch) and a little maple syrup.

Fine is an author and hemp farmer, but he introduces himself as a goat rancher. His ranch is forty-two acres, with half an acre dedicated to a garden that mostly grows the food that feeds his family, but he also cultivates hemp varieties to use in his own product fields (located elsewhere) and in his advisory work. "We plant polyculture style, so mostly growing for food and a little bit for seed development. If I'm liking what I see, I'll build that seed stock on other farms growing elsewhere." He describes a patch of hemp in the "tomato part of our garden" that is so tangled "I can't tell who's supporting whom." He suggests the hemp helps the other crops – "watermelon has done better this year than ever before" – alongside basil and sunflowers.

Fine farms regeneratively. "We're all soil farmers now," he says. "Anyone who plants anything from a backyard garden to thousands of acres of any agricultural crop is a soil farmer first and foremost." According to Fine, building healthy soil is important because it sequesters carbon and allows us to produce enough healthy food, both of which are vital to humanity's long-term survival. For Fine, the regenerative model also needs to make sure farmers are financially rewarded for laboring on the land. He wants to see them have some ownership over the product that goes to market, rather than simply selling it as a raw material to a company that will add value through processing. He advocates for cooperatives to enable knowledge sharing between farmers, so they know the best growing practices in their region and can cooperate to add value to the raw materials produced on their land through processing and manufacturing. "My whole idea of regenerative is as much about how people are treated as it is about how the earth is treated," he explains.

He holds a stalk of hemp fiber in his hand. It is pale and dry, with strips dangling from the central woody stem. He waves the stalk and tells me the strips on the outside are the bast fiber part of the plant, used to make textiles, rope, and next-generation plastics and supercapacitors. To create high-quality textiles, you have to grow bast fiber variety hemp, and it needs certain qualities, such as wide spacing between the nodes on the plant to allow for longer fibers and smoother fabrics. For certain types of textiles, the ideal fiber will be long and thin – with distinctions sometimes even measured down to the micron. Fine explains that after hemp has been harvested, processing it requires some scientific knowledge, from retting it in the field to getting it to a processing facility that has the equipment to take textile-grade fiber through the many stages of its manufacturing. This is where it gets tricky; while the processing infrastructure exists in Europe and China, there is a gap in the United States, so American farmers growing hemp for textile fiber don't have anywhere to process it locally.

Fine says the industry in the United States needs a few things: large-scale investment in factories or equipment that can process hemp from fiber through to fabric; the accumulation of knowledge so these facilities can be staffed by skilled operators; and enough hemp fiber to make the investment in the factories and equipment worthwhile. Growing hemp for fiber requires a lot of acreage. Fine estimates it would take 3,100 acres, at a minimum, to feed a very small $3–5 million facility all year. However, he is optimistic about the challenges he outlines, none of which is insurmountable. The other thing to keep in mind is the quality of hemp needed for textiles. It's a specialty crop and to get the right fiber quality, you have to know what you're doing, which can be tricky in a place like the USA, where every hemp farmer is new to the game.

This is where being a soil farmer comes in, Fine says. "'The good news is, when you are cultivating and nurturing beneficial micro-organisms in the soil before you plant, whatever your product, it will be better quality if the soil is healthy." Soil cultivation is an art and science that should be specific to the region and will depend on what crops or plants were grown on the land in the past. Fine describes cultivating his own soils by going into the hills above his watershed in the spring and collecting mycelium strains of fungus and old dead wood chunks from muddy, watery areas. He uses this debris to make a compost tea that he adds to the soil to help increase its local fungal content. If this is done regularly, the soil tends to retain good fungal content, so you don't have to do it as much every year. He also applies a mixture of goat poop (from the ranch) and organic alfalfa to build nitrogen and foster other healthy critters like earthworms. He adds trace minerals from diluted ocean kelp that he sources from people who harvest it regeneratively. Over winter, when he's not planting hemp, he plants soil-fixing, nitrogen-building crops like clover and vegetables. By doing these things, Fine ensures the soil has a healthy microbial balance. "If those critters underground are happy, it'll be reflected in the health of the crop you're growing," he explains. Hemp also helps build the soil, Fine says, "Because it has long, strong tap roots, it plays an important role in aerating the soil," especially soil that has become compacted through overuse or harsh monoculture treatment.

Once the soil has been cultivated, if you're planting for fiber hemp, there should be five-inch spacing between the seeds, "as opposed to ganja style, which requires five feet." The seeds are planted at a half-inch depth and shouldn't need too much watering. In a few months, the hemp will have grown to its full height and be ready for harvesting. Hemp is usually planted as a monocrop, which is not as good for the health of the soil as multi-species planting. "You definitely can companion plant with hemp," Fine tells me, "but it has to be done right" – and the best combination will vary depending on the region. As for cover crops, which are planted in between harvests to improve the health of the soil, you "may or may not want your over-winter crop growing to fruition. It might do its job as a nitrogen fixer before then, so you can plow it under and turn it into green mulch, and the soil will be ready for the main crop or the cash crop."

The other big arm of regenerative agriculture is integrating animals and livestock among the crops. On large commercial acreage, many farmers are implementing rotational grazing techniques, but on Fine's small home hemp field, "it's about trying to keep our hungry, hemp-loving goats *out* of the field. We do bring them treats from all sides of the plant and add hemp seed to their feed." He says he's heard of farms that run chickens through their hemp fields but on his ranch, the only animals integrated into the farming process are the goats. "The role of my goats – I say my goats, but they think I'm their goat – is their poop goes on the ground to help the soil."

After the hemp is harvested, whatever remains of the crop has to be plowed into the soil, except on small-acre farms that utilize no-till techniques and can plant around earlier harvests. Fine insists that most hemp farmers "use low-till, but it's not exactly no-till." There are some innovations happening in this space, including research to see whether the parts of the plant left over from processing, like the herd and the stalks, can be put back into the field to use as cover and replenish some of the lost nutrients.

Since the Farm Bill was passed in 2018, there has been something of a hemp renaissance across the USA, but when it comes to fiber reaching the real-world marketplace, Fine says, "processing infrastructure is the undeniable bottleneck." He believes in hemp as a future fiber and tells me about its amazing qualities, from fiber to soil. He even thinks being on the field, among the hemp plants, can make you happier. "Every mammal has an endocannabinoid system," he says (this is the complex cell-signaling system that plays a role in regulating sleep, appetite, mood, memory, and fertility). "When I'm out in the hemp field and I'm breathing in terpenes that make the plant smell nice, I'm triggering my endocannabinoid system, and it really does makes me happy."

Alexandra La Pierre is a carefully spoken materials developer at Patagonia who describes herself as the company's unofficial global point of contact for hemp. She tells me China is currently the largest exporter of hemp, and home to the global leading experts in hemp technology. According to Textile Exchange, China is also the world's main producer of hemp fiber.[5] Although there is no official data available for China's hemp production, the United States Department of Agriculture estimated the Chinese hemp market was worth US$1.7 billion in 2017, and fiber accounts for roughly seventy-five percent of this.[6] However, hemp fiber still makes up a very small percentage of the global textile market (0.2 percent)[7] – Textile Exchange estimates hemp had an annual production of 60,657 metric tons in 2019, compared to 868,374 metric tons of flax and 26 million metric tons of cotton.

Patagonia has an ongoing partnership with Hemp Fortex, one of the world's main hemp fiber suppliers, which still operates out of the province Jill Dumain visited almost thirty years ago.[8] They source hemp fiber from a network of farmer co-ops and turn it into knitted and woven fabrics that are purchased by companies like Patagonia. La Pierre describes a visit to Hemp Fortex's processing facilities, where the hemp is transformed from woody stalk to smooth fabric. She says they've been doing it such a long time, they make it look more like an art form than a traditional textile process.

The farmers working with Hemp Fortex are in the process of transitioning into organic farming. "We're working with co-ops of farmers that are interested in growing organically," La Pierre says. "The next step will be having conversations around whether those farms are willing to do 'organic plus' and move in the direction of regenerative farming." She describes hemp as "uniquely positioned" for regenerative agriculture because "it is already set up to be organically grown in a lot of places."

Once hemp is ready to be harvested, large-scale farms use a specialized tractor with a blade that flips the hemp on its side and slices through the woody hemp stalk approximately five inches off the ground. On smaller farms, plants are pulled from the root by hand. The long stalks lie in rows along the field, where they will be left to ret, like flax. La Pierre says this process takes advantage of the natural microbiomes in the field to degrade the fiber and the stalk. The stalks are then bundled into bales and taken to a facility where they are stripped of their outer shell in a mechanical process known as decortication. "Sometimes, this is called skutching," says La Pierre. "It's essentially breaking that outside shell of the hemp stalk, and that woody piece at the core is also going to get broken down. You're crushing everything so that the wood falls away from the fiber." Then the fibers are degummed, which is a wet process using caustic soda to break down the lignin and pectin holding the fibers to the stalk, so that the individual fibers become separated. As La Pierre explains, degumming involves cooking the plant; this is the most water- and energy-intensive part of the process, although it is only necessary to achieve very fine, lightweight textiles. In Europe, they tend to opt for hemp fabrics with a more natural feel that haven't undergone degumming.

The fibers are then heckled by dragging them through large combs or spears to separate, straighten, and clean them, which results in hair-like fibers that are ready to spin. These are flung around to shake out the excess pulp before tying them into bundles. By this stage, the fibers look coarse and golden, like a cross between horsehair and strands of straw. They are then run through a machine to help further separate the strands before being spun into yarn. Once it has been spun, hemp is silvery and soft and curls in long hackles around itself. From here, it is strung across massive looms and woven into fabric.

Hemp growing represents interesting opportunities for American farmers and, in response, Patagonia has launched its "Bring Hemp Home" program. The program aims to facilitate conversations between farmers, legislative bodies, and standards committees to figure out how to create an American hemp supply chain that can "move from plant all the way through to processing." The project has three main goals: to elevate and raise awareness of industrial hemp; to increase the amount of hemp being grown in the United States; and to help build hemp-processing infrastructure.

La Pierre acknowledges that they're learning as they go. After the 2018 Farm Bill passed, she says, farmers were enthusiastic. "At the beginning, a lot of people were taking seed and saying 'we're going to grow hemp.'" Many didn't understand the market or how many steps it takes to turn a hemp crop into a textile that a company like Patagonia might buy. Often, the farmers would come directly to Patagonia with bales of unprocessed hemp and she'd have to explain that "this is just not how we're set up."

Patagonia's role is to help solve problems that can't be tackled by just one sector of the supply chain. "I get a lot of calls from people in the industry who don't have a textiles background," La Pierre says. "They come to me and say: we have stalks, or we have bales of hemp, we can decorticate them, but who's the degummer? Or we grew hemp fiber … what do we do with it?" Patagonia is trying to bring people and organizations together to establish supply chain processes, whether that's by directly working with a farmer or connecting a farmer who has grown hemp fiber with a spinner to find out if the quality of the crop is good enough to do a trial with one of the company's weaving or knitting partners. Since some of the processing stages are similar to those for wool and cotton, it's possible to repurpose old wool or cotton mills, although hemp can only be processed in a wool or cotton mill after it has under-gone hemp-specific processes such as decortication.

As Doug Fine articulated, people are an important consideration in regenerative farming – and Patagonia agrees. La Pierre describes the social aspect and the well-being of the farmers or producers of hemp as part of their planning, so they can ensure a "livable wage for the farmer." She says it starts with defining expectations on the market side, with proper grading systems so that "farmers know the quality of hemp that they're shooting for, and know they can get the price they're asking for at the end." Developing knowledge and systems to ensure the work of the farmers is properly remunerated is where a lot of the work remains to be done.

Given that the hemp industry is still in its infancy in both the United States and China, there is enormous potential for growth, which is per-haps part of the reason hemp has earned a reputation as a fiber of the future. La Pierre says she hears hemp described as a "savior fiber" but despite this, "there are very clear places where hemp processing can ben-efit from innovation." Thankfully, she says, there are people working on it. "What I'm most excited about is seeing how we make this fiber – which we know, when it's growing in the soil, is doing this work to help benefit the climate. How do we get the processing to match? Because if we can do that, it could be a really beautiful thing for the industry, and I have a lot of hope that we're going to get there."

This thinking is echoed globally: farming hemp benefits nature and the soil, but to grow it at a scale that can have significant impact on climate change and landscapes, it needs to be commercially viable, and the hemp produced needs to be suitable for manufacturing. To achieve this, the processing arm requires innovations. Farmers in France, the second larg-est producer of hemp in the world, plant it before they plant flax because it suppresses weeds and leaves behind a totally clean field. Because it has a one-hundred-day growing season, it can be effectively rotated with other cash crops to maximize farmers' cash returns. European hemp farmers are already embracing technical innovations to eliminate harsh chemicals and minimize the energy required by mechanical defibring. In *Fibershed*, Rebecca Burgess describes working on ecologically focused solutions for degumming, including enzymes, recycled water baths, compressed liquid carbon dioxide, and UV light treatments.[9]

Though hemp currently represents a tiny portion of the fiber industry, it has enormous potential. And it illustrates the three different aspects of making clothes that must come together if fashion is to become truly sustainable. The first is farming fiber in ways that support the land – which hemp has great potential to do both because of its innate characteristics and through the continued education of farmers willing to embrace regenerative techniques.

The second is using best practices in processing, including renewable power sources, closed-loop processes, or other careful management of chemicals and waste, alongside fair wages and working conditions for the people working in the factories – things Patagonia is researching and tackling through its partnership with Hemp Fortex.

The third is less clear-cut: moving away from centralized offshore manufacturing and returning to local industry. It is something that comes up again and again in regenerative fashion conversations, from wool to flax to cotton. In a perfect world, fiber processing and textile manufacturing would never have become centralized in Asia. Local industries all over the world would still be thriving; the knowledge and skills to process the produce of local farms would not have been forgotten; mills would have remained operational with technology and techniques that continued to advance; and the unchecked exploitation of people and the environment would never have happened.

But unfortunately, we cannot start to solve these issues in the past; we have to make decisions based on where we are. And right now, China is the dominant producer of textiles in the world. It has immense capacity to process raw fiber; its infrastructure and facilities dwarf those available elsewhere; and it has a knowledgeable and highly skilled workforce. Some Chinese companies are at the forefront of regenerative agriculture and best-practice processing – and, of course, some are not. The forced labor of the Uyghurs is one particularly alarming example of human rights abuses occurring along fashion's supply chains, exacerbated by the lack of transparency in a country with an opaque political system.

In addition, the pandemic revealed how vulnerable the globalized world is to disrupted supply chains, disruptions that are likely to become more common as the climate becomes less stable. It makes sense for farmers and Communities to have at least some production close to the fields where food and fiber is being grown, to ensure they are always able to turn their product into something they can sell and so the community always has access to its own supply of goods. But the reality is, to build or rebuild the infrastructure and train people to process even the tiniest percentage of China's textile output would (in most instances) take ten to twenty years. Another consideration when advocating for a return to localized production is the knowledge and skill it takes to produce beautiful, high-quality garments and textiles. These things cannot be compromised as we reshape the industry, because they are key to subverting the take-make-waste model of consumption. A return to local production has to ensure this skill and knowledge, the artisan's appreciation of beauty and artistic sensibility, are captured and safeguarded.

So the smartest thing to do is take a multipronged approach: encourage best practices and transparency in existing manufacturing and processing facilities, while laying the groundwork for a return to local industry. That means boosting both private and public investment in local infrastructure; legislating to support this, perhaps including the reintroduction of tariffs on imported goods; and encouraging training all over the world. What better time than now to start decentralizing fashion's supply chains and look forward to a very different future for the fashion industry?

CHAPTER 10

True-blue Recycled Denim and the Isle of Wight

I bought my favorite pair of jeans at a thrift shop in a seaside town. They are vintage Rip Curl (a surf brand), but they're cut like classic Levi's 501s. The previous owner wrote his name in green inside the waistband. They have a deep high rise, five pockets, silver rivets, twin stitching, and a straight leg. They're made of thick denim and when they come out of the wash, they are so stiff and rigid it's very satisfying to pull them on and feel them wrap around my hips and waist as I zip them up. But it is their color I love the most, a faded true blue. It's pretty but strong, darker around the seams. A soft blue, like an early morning sky. It goes with everything. White tank tops, silk shirts, black tailored blazers, navy overcoats, brightly colored knitwear. The universality of jeans remains an enigma to the fashion industry; no other item of clothing has been so consistently in style since its inception.

Denim is a one hundred percent cotton woven twill fabric, made with one colored and one white thread. Its origins are convoluted. The town of Nime, France, is often cited as denim's birthplace, the word supposedly a contraction of the French *de Nime*, which translates to *of Nime*. But the fabric made there, *Serge de Nime*, was a wool blend while denim has always been made of cotton. Another cotton twill, confusingly called jean, was manufactured in Genoa in the sixteenth century, but it differed from denim as it was made of two yarns of the same color. By the eighteenth century, both denim and jean were being manufactured by the English, who liked to apply French names to their fabrics to make them more appealing, and perhaps this is how the cotton twill made from blue and white yarn got its name. Both fabrics were extremely popular by the time the Americans are known to have manufactured them, and throughout the nineteenth century, jean and denim were distinguished by the garments made from them: jean was used for fine trousers and denim for workwear.

This is where the story of denim jeans, as we know them today, really begins. It has been mythologized in the history of both the United States and fashion – the daring immigrant who arrived in a new land, worked hard, spotted a gap in the market, and invented something that has become so ingrained in the psyche of modern society it's hard to imagine life without it. What would we wear if we wanted to look cool had Levi Strauss never made denim "waist overalls" more durable by reinforcing the tension points with little copper rivets?

Strauss, an immigrant from Bavaria who changed his name to Levi from Loeb, opened a dry goods store in San Francisco in 1853 where he sold blankets, cloth by the yard, and clothing. In 1872, he was approached by a tailor named Jacob Davis, who bought blue denim from Strauss to cut and sew waist overalls. In response to complaints his pants were not durable enough for the miners who worked in them, Davis reinforced them with copper rivets, an amendment so popular he wanted to patent it. The patent fee was $68, which was a big sum for a business of his size but a relatively manageable one for someone of Strauss's stature. He offered Strauss fifty percent of the business if he would cover the patent fee. The patent was granted in 1873, and soon after, Levi Strauss & Company opened its first San Francisco factory to manufacture blue jeans using denim from the Amoskeag Manufacturing Company in New Hampshire. Imitations came fast, and in 1927, a competitor, Lee, replaced the button fly with a hookless fastener – or zip, as we know it today.

By 1929, Levi was selling $4.2 million worth of stock a year, in part thanks to the Wild West taking hold of Americans' imagination. Denim jeans had an everyman appeal that paired well with Americans' fascination with adventure on the frontier. By the middle of the century, denim had become synonymous with Hollywood and rebels, youth and freedom. Jeans were worn by poets, hippies, and movie stars, from John Wayne to Marlon Brando, Marilyn Monroe to Jack Kerouac. By the 1980s, when Brooke Shields purred into the camera that nothing came between her and her Calvin Klein jeans, the fashion industry and the world were completely in the thrall of this single item of clothing and everything it seemed to promise. Up until this point, jeans had to be worn in the bathtub so they shrank to fit the contours of the body, and fading and rips were hard won by hard wearing. But synthetics, changes in manufacturing, and the rise of fast fashion saw the denim industry undergo rapid transformation, causing jeans to shed their origin as a working man's pant. Waist overalls were subject to the whims of an ever-accelerating trend cycle; they morphed into pants that were skinny or ripped, stoned washed or high waisted, streaked or low rise. According to Maxine Bedat, who chronicled the environmental cost of a pair of jeans in her book *Unravelled*, between 1993 and 2003, two hundred new brands selling denim products entered the market.[1]

Levi's sales peaked at US$7.1 billion in 1996, a few years into this rapid expansion. But just over a year later, the company began closing its American facilities, purportedly to cut costs, as denim became increasingly ubiquitous and competition increasingly fierce. In 1999, Levi's started moving production offshore, citing the pressure of competing with rivals who manufactured in Asia or Mexico, where labor costs were cheaper. By 2004, all its American facilities were closed.[2] A shifting media landscape meant consumers had become influenced by marketing campaigns, cooler designer jeans, and cheaper mass-market options. When Levi's closed the last of its American factories, it told *The New York Times* it was so it could invest more in promoting its product.[3] This marked a change in its business structure that was mirrored across the United States. Levi's went from a company that made American jeans from American cotton in American factories to a company that marketed and sold the idea of American denim. All of this was exacerbated by the rising popularity of free trade agreements that removed tariffs on imported goods and saw a decline in local production take hold across much of the West. Values shifted away from considering where and how things were made to focusing on branding and price points, a trend that would ramp up over the next two decades as large companies continued to outsource production to countries with fewer protections for workers and the environment. In the 1960s, just five percent of clothing worn by Americans was made in Japan, Hong Kong, Pakistan, and India. By the 1970s, the number was twenty-five percent, and today, more than ninety-eight percent of Americans' clothes are made overseas.[4]

In 2020, with reported sales of just over US$4.45 billion, Levi's still has the largest share of the denim jeans market, which is globally worth around $63.5 billion.[5] China is the leading exporter of denim fabric; in fact, China is now the dominant manufacturer of textiles globally. According to Bedat, in the twelve months after July 2019, China made 45.86 billion meters of fabric. In 2018, it had 37.6 percent of the global market – more than six times the second largest exporter, India, which had just six percent. She goes on to say that manufacturing a pair of jeans in El Paso, Texas, (a former location of Levi's factories) would have cost $7, while in China it costs as little as $1.50.[6]

As production moved offshore, the volume of clothes being produced and consumed continued to skyrocket and consumers' expectations of quality were reshaped to match the cheap, trend-driven products on offer. Meanwhile, the media infiltrated further into our lives, all the way to the devices in our pockets, and narratives of newness and recreational shopping took hold. We were delivered an increasingly fast cycle of more, based on false wants and promises. And so, the denim jean, which was literally invented to be hard wearing, became an item that could be bought, worn a few times, and disposed of. According to Dana Thomas, author of *Fashionopolis*, the average American buys four new pairs of jeans each year.[7] But it's not just Americans: all over the world, we are buying more clothes, wearing them less, and throwing them away. Data from 2015 suggests 1.25 billion pairs of jeans are sold every year (although some sources suggest the number is closer to 2 billion). According to a 2017 report by the Ellen MacArthur Foundation, clothing production doubled between 2000 and 2015, and the number of times garments were worn declined by thirty-six percent. Consumers purchased sixty percent more garments and discarded them twice as fast. The result is a world where tons and tons of textiles are landfilled or incinerated every second.

The Ellen MacArthur Foundation's headquarters are located on a tiny island off the south coast of the United Kingdom called the Isle of Wight. To get there, you can take the train from London to Southhampton, catch a bus to the port and from there, take a passenger ferry for twenty-five minutes to the sailing port town called Cowes. The architecture is typically British: double-story buildings with bay windows built from gray-brown bricks, occasionally painted pastel pink, yellow, or blue. Lines of bunting run in zigzags between the rooftops, and tiny boats zip up and down the River Medina, which separates the east and west banks of the village. The foundation is across the river and only accessible via chain-link ferry. Catching a boat to the headquarters door is a fitting detail, since its founder, Dame Ellen MacArthur, once held the world record for the fastest solo sailor to circumnavigate the globe in a yacht.

After spending seventy-one days alone at sea, she returned with a new understanding of the fragility of the planet and the limit to the earth's finite resources. She created the Ellen MacArthur Foundation, a charity dedicated to promoting and developing the idea of a circular economy across various sectors, including fashion. A circular economy reimagines our current modes of manufacturing and disposal, so that new products are generated from materials already in circulation, essentially from waste. Broadly speaking, the principles of circularity are: eliminate waste and pollution; keep products and materials in use; and regenerate natural systems. At the Copenhagen Fashion Summit in 2017, where the foundation launched its *A New Textiles Economy* report, MacArthur described to the audience of designers, buyers, writers, academics, and consultants the foundation's plan to create a circular economy for fashion.

The foundation's circular economy for fashion has three pillars. The first is simply that products should be used more. The second pillar is that products should be "made to be made again" or be designed and constructed in a way that ensures they can be reused, remade, and recycled. Finally, after a vigorous, long life of use, repair, and recycling, garments must be composted and returned to the earth.

Theoretically, this makes perfect sense and, in a way, it seems ridiculous to describe it as an ambitious vision for the future. Unfortunately, built-in obsolescence is firmly entrenched in modern society, and fashion has strayed a long way from valuing quality over quantity. The concept seems simple, an easy return to a time when clothes were designed to be loved and used for as long as possible – like my favorite Rip Curl jeans – before being safely recycled. But the reality of applying the principles of circularity to fashion's intricate supply chain is more complicated, and so the foundation thought it would be a good idea to road-test the principles by making a fully circular garment. In 2019, they decided to start with a pair of jeans.

Speaking to me from a white room in her home on the Isle of Wight, Laura Balmond is the lead of Make Fashion Circular, the arm of the Ellen MacArthur Foundation that created the Jeans Redesign project. She has long brown hair, a soft English accent, and apologizes because she caught a cold at a recent conference, although she assures me it isn't COVID-19. She tells me the project was born of a desire to move beyond conversations about what might or might not be possible and apply the theories of circularity to a real product. She says jeans were an obvious choice "because they're iconic, so many people wear them, and most organizations already had them in their portfolio." As well as being universal, they are also quite polluting, so they were a good place to start. "The way they are made uses huge amounts of water along with various different dyes and chemistry," she says. There was also already work being done along the supply chain to improve their environmental impacts, such as changes to energy and water use.

Levi's began conducting life cycle assessments (LCAs) of its jeans in 2007 and has since made strides in reducing its water and energy use. The company dedicated a 2015 report, *Life Cycle of a Jean*, to the environmental impact of a pair of 501s. Calculating the impact of any garment is very complicated, and jeans are no different. For example, you may have read that it takes 20,000 liters of water to produce the kilogram of cotton required for a pair of jeans. This statistic is hard to verify, but it pops up again and again. Seven thousand liters is another common estimate, while Levi's places the figure at 3,781 liters, including 2,565 liters to grow the fiber. The discrepancies are, in part, because the water required to irrigate cotton will vary from farm to farm and between bioregions.

Denim's other environmental impacts include the pesticides used to grow cotton and the pollution of waterways by harmful chemicals such as azo dyes – a group of chemicals banned by the European Union and considered hazardous if they come into direct contact with the skin. Then there are the air miles traveled by the cotton as it morphs from boll to yarn to textile to denim. Each process can take place on a different continent, not to mention the large amounts of energy required at the factories where these processes are undertaken. Finally, more energy and chemicals are expended to make new jeans look lived-in and worn. To achieve these looks, several techniques are applied to literally distress and damage new denim before the jeans are sold, including sandblasting, bleaching, pumicing with stones, and distressing jeans by hand with sandpaper. Each one consumes more energy and puts the health of factory workers at risk.

In recognition of the complexities of this supply chain, the Ellen MacArthur Foundation brought together a group of denim experts to develop a vision of what best practice looks like for a pair of jeans. These brands, manufacturers, fabric mills, collectors, recyclers, and academics developed guidelines to design and produce jeans in accordance with the principles of a circular economy. Balmond says, "When we started to dive in and understand what the challenges are today with the design of jeans and look at what would make them more fit for a circular economy, we realized the level of complexity." The first version of the report was published in 2019; in 2020, the guidelines were revised to the final three: in a circular economy, jeans would be used more, jeans would be made to be made again, and jeans would be made from safe and recycled or renewable inputs.

The first of these principles – use jeans more – seems like a fairly straightforward place to start. Increasing the number of times something is worn creates value and reduces waste. The foundation investigated the durability of the average pair of jeans and found two things.

First, despite once being a workwear item, the durability of jeans had significantly reduced over time. And second, there was no consistently used method or baseline across the fashion industry to measure and compare the durability of garments. They found that some companies test for performance indicators like tensile strength, abrasion resistance, and color fastness – but because there is no consistency across these measurements, the foundation felt they had to establish some standards.

They soon discovered that some organizations were only testing jeans for one wash cycle, which gave no indication of their durability. They needed tests that would account for a more ambitious life cycle, so they asked manufacturers to increase their durability testing for a minimum of thirty home laundries. "That doesn't mean the jeans just had to withstand thirty home washes," Balmond clarifies. What it means is that after thirty home washes, the manufacturers had to perform their normal durability testing before the jeans left the factory. "They should still be in as-new condition – that was our minimum criteria for durability." The onus was also placed on businesses to provide consumers with information on how to care for jeans, including by washing them less frequently, washing them at lower temperatures, and avoiding tumble drying. These instructions needed to be clearly visible and attached to the jeans themselves, not on a swing tag. Finally, the jeans should be made available through business models that encouraged use and reuse options such as rental and resale.

The second principle – jeans should be made to be made again – required the design process to account for the repairability and recyclability of a garment. The foundation drew on research from its 2017 report and interviews with multiple recycling specialists. As the circular economy insists that products and materials be kept in use and cared for to retain their value, they needed to know how different materials fared through the recycling process. Balmond says, "The rule is, if you're designing and making a product, you should ensure that one hundred percent of the materials in that product can be disassembled, taken back, and eventually put into a recycling process that can produce a product of a high quality."

The guidelines set out three different types of textile recycling. Fiber recycling is performed by sorting textiles by color and material, shredding them, and spinning them back into fibers. Polymer recycling uses chemistry to take the fibers back to their polymer level by destroying them but keeping the chemical structure intact, either by melting and extruding them or using a chemical solvent. The third method, chemical monomer recycling, breaks the material down into smaller individual particles that can serve as feedstock to produce virgin-quality particles. Balmond describes the main distinction as "mechanical versus chemical" – that is, fiber recycling versus polymer and chemical monomer recycling.

The conversations with textile recyclers revealed that recycled fabrics do best when materials are made from a single type of fiber. Balmond says this initially seemed like it would be really simple because jeans were traditionally made of one hundred percent cotton. "But because of the style and comfort, there's a lot of elastane and polyester mixed in with the cotton, and it becomes really difficult for the recycling technologies to separate out and put it back into something of high quality." In most fabric recycling, blended materials like cotton and polyester require an extra process because the cellulose has to be separated from the synthetic material before recycling can occur, and this often results in waste. So they set a requirement that the jeans had to include a minimum of ninety-eight percent cellulose-based fibers like cotton, hemp, linen, lyocell, modal, and viscose, with mono-materials being given priority over blends. The ninety-eight percent metric covered the entire garment – including the fabric, interlinings, pockets, and labels – except for the hardware, and allowed room for the manufacturers to use synthetic threads (although cellulose ones were recommended).

The next recommendation to ensure recyclability was that any hardware added to the jeans like buttons, zips, or rivets had to be easy to disassemble. Balmond tells me she was shocked when the recyclers told her that usually "the whole top of the pair of jeans gets cut off completely and doesn't even make it into the recycling because the rivets, the pockets, the stitching are made of so many different components that it's easier to just chop it off and throw it away." The rivets famously added and patented by Levi's in 1873 posed a particular problem for recyclers, so the guidelines recommended that rivets not be used at all – much to the dismay of the designers who were aware of their role in history.

To ensure easy collection and sorting, the jeans had to be correctly labeled, with their materials clearly listed and a marker identifying them as part of the Jeans Redesign Project. For transparency and traceability, the guidelines recommend this information be made available using digital technology like blockchain, QR codes, traceable fiber technology, and RFID tags. This reflects one of the issues with textile recycling; identifying the different fibers correctly is critical to the recycling process, but currently this relies on manual identification. But innovations are on their way. Evrnu, a textile innovations company in Seattle, has spent the last seven years developing technology that can accurately identify the different fibers in a garment using artificial intelligence and deep scanning to sort fibers quickly and, with very high precision, depolymerize them and turn them back into the supply chain.

The third guideline is: jeans are made from safe and recycled or renewable inputs. The jeans must be produced in a way that is safe for the long-term health of people and ecosystems. They have to be made with chemicals that comply with the Zero Discharge of Hazardous Chemicals Restricted Substances List – a list of chemical substances banned from intentional use in facilities that process textiles. A circular economy requires that dangerous substances must be eliminated to allow for safe recirculation of materials. The guidelines ban several chemical processes, including conventional electroplating metals, stone washing (used to fade jeans), oxidizing finishing agents like potassium permanagate, and sand blasting (used to make denim look distressed). It also stipulates that fabric mills implement wastewater guidelines, including testing and reporting, and that the water volume used for denim fabric is a maximum of 30 liters per meter.

The final stipulation for the jeans is that they be made from cellulose-based fibers that come from regenerative, organic, or transitional methods. This means natural fibers like cotton and hemp, or man-made cellulose fibers like lyocell from farming practices that build soil health and carbon content and improve water cycles, biodiversity, and the resilience of the surrounding ecosystem. In acknowledgement that it's currently difficult to source regenerative natural fibers because it is not yet a widespread practice, the guidelines allow for sourcing from transitional organic methods and use certifications like the Global Organic Textile Standard or the Organic Content Standard. For man-made cellulose like viscose, they use Canopy's Hot Button Ranking, which ensures the viscose was not sourced from ancient or endangered forests.

The Ellen MacArthur Foundation considered alternatives to cellulose fibers, Balmond says. "We did have some slightly silly debates about making the jeans out of one hundred percent recycled polyester … would that also be fine because then they could be recycled as a mono-material and that could work – but there's obviously some issues." One concern was that polyester jeans would be awful to wear. Another was the issue of microfiber pollution. When a synthetic garment is put through a washing machine, it sheds plastic microfibers that end up in our oceans, rivers, and soil. The number of plastic microfibers entering the ocean by 2050 could exceed 22 million tons. And alarmingly, in 2022, scientists in The Netherlands found microplastic pollution in the blood of eighty percent of the people they tested.[8] Balmond says microfiber pollution might be fixable with innovations on the textile side. "It's a really difficult one, but it does come down to the design. If it causes pollution through microfibers or chemistry, how do you redesign that product to not cause that pollution? Can you change the fiber structure? For instance, using a filament versus a staple can make a big difference in terms of the amount of shedding." But ultimately, she says, polyester comes from oil, which is a finite, non-renewable resource, and the foundation champions regenerative, renewable materials.

Some of the metrics were easier to meet than others. For example, ninety percent of participants were able to source organic cotton, but many reported market availability and price as barriers to scaling. Almost all participants reported struggling to identify and source cellulose-based fibers that had been produced using regenerative agriculture – a sign of how new the movement is. Regardless, of the seventy-two organizations that participated in the Jeans Redesign Project, eighty percent successfully made denim or jeans that complied with the project guidelines. By the end of May 2021, more than half a million pairs of redesigned jeans had been put on the market and, Balmond proudly tells me, most of them sold out.

This meant the foundation was able to demonstrate proof of concept – that their vision for a circular fashion industry, for circular denim, could work ... up to a point. For the concept to be fully realized, the jeans produced through the project will need to be collected, sorted, and recycled after years of use and wear. This is possible in theory, but textile recycling systems are still in their infancy. In *A New Textiles Economy*, the foundation reported that less than one percent of textile waste was being recycled into new clothing, with US$100 billion worth of materials going to waste every year. More recent estimates suggest the amount of textile waste being recycled into new garments could be as little as 0.07 percent.[9]

Conversations about textile waste are becoming more and more main-stream. Inside and outside the fashion industry, governments and companies are beginning to understand that the precious resources textile waste contains represent an opportunity to generate new tex-tiles, solve the issue of rising landfills, and replace some of the demand for virgin resources. The European Union is currently working on leg-islation to manage and control textile waste, and undoubtedly the rest of the world will soon follow. On average, Europeans consume 26 kilograms of textiles each a year, and discard 11. Under the European Commission's Waste Framework Directive, by 2025, member states will have to set up separate collections for textiles. What to do with the waste poses another issue; even countries with high textile col-lection rates, such as Germany, are still shipping much of it to devel-oping countries.[10] The commission plans to study the environmental effectiveness of textile recycling with a view to providing guidance on innovation in the sector.

Several private companies, in the US, UK, and Australia, have devel-oped successful pilot programs that can turn used textiles back into new textiles. But to be effective, the textile recycling sector requires expan-sion across three areas: collection of textile waste in a manner similar to the way waste streams like paper or glass are managed; sorting of textile waste by fiber types; and construction of recycling plants capable of pro-cessing waste at a high volume. Given the sheer volume of textile waste, everything has to happen on a vast scale.

One of the biggest innovators in the textile recycling space is Seattle company Evrnu. Christopher Stanev, the company's chief technology officer, speaks slowly with an Eastern European accent. He is a textile engineering and chemistry expert who holds numerous patents for his inventions in textile technologies. Before founding Evrnu with his col-league Stacey Flynn, he held various leadership positions in technical innovation at companies including Nike and Target.

Evrnu is focused on creating high-performance materials from dis-carded clothing. One of these innovations, NuCycl, takes discarded clothing, breaks it down and uses repolymerization to convert the orig-inal fiber molecules into new, high-quality textiles that can be recycled again and again. A crude explanation of the process is that the fab-ric is sorted, shredded, and stripped of dyes and prints, leaving behind only cellulose. The cellulose is purified and turned into a pulp, which is turned into thick paper. The paper is then dissolved in a solvent and, through a process of heat, extrusion, and spinning, it is turned into lyo-cell – a type of rayon. The company works with a number of different materials, including recycled polyester, but Stanev emphasizes the work they have done on regenerated cellulosic fibers. For example, they can convert the cotton from a used garment into a cellulose fiber, like lyo-cell, that is normally derived from trees. Stanev says, "We are making fibers from recycled cotton, melted and extruded in a shape and form that mimics and outperforms the polyester or nylon of today."

He says they focus on the recycling of cellulosic fibers for a num-ber of reasons. One is a preference for natural materials over synthetics because of concerns about microfiber pollution and the harm caused by garments that don't biodegrade. "Nature is designed to break cellulose down," Stanev says. "It knows how to deal with it." Using the cellulose from cotton, "you can extrude fiber with the same or better perfor-mance, and you can do it multiple times. If the natural fibers do shed, they will disappear, similar to the biomass and the weeds that fall in the river and go into the ocean." He advocates for polyester textile waste to be captured and used in the construction of cars and insulation – things that are easy to recover and don't leak into water systems.

Their preference for natural fibers also relates to performance. Natu-ral fibers, Stanev says, make clothes that are more absorbent and com-fortable. Their technology allows them to design cellulosic materials that are moisture-wicking and mimic the performance of synthetic materials usually found in athletics gear. "We have been working with a performance lab to develop materials that can replace the performance of polyester and nylon very successfully … cellulosic fibers perform well with moisture removal; they are cool when it's hot and warm when it's cold outside, which is not the same with fibers that are made from oil." He says the polymers from cotton perform better than those from trees because cotton is higher in cellulose content. "Cotton polymers are longer, stronger, more lustrous, and softer to touch against the skin. So any fiber that is made from cotton instead of pulp derived from trees ends up being more attractive, more comfortable, and more durable."

Their third reason for prioritizing cellulosic fibers is the amount of cotton waste that already exists. "Every year, there are 24 or 25 million tons of cotton produced and, twenty-five years down the road, this ends up in landfill or is incinerated," Stanev explains.[11] He sees recycled material as an important replacement for viscose rayon, which is consuming millions of tons of cellulose from trees. "Instead of cutting down trees, let's collect the cotton we have, because there is three times more cotton that goes into landfill or is incinerated."

Stanev's voice becomes animated when he explains that as well as performing better, fabric made from regenerated cellulose can itself be recycled. "We believe we can recycle the polymers multiple times, and when there's a point we can't use them as a fiber anymore, we can turn it into packaging boxes, paper, or construction materials." He points out that "all gold that's ever been sourced is still in circulation – it gets melted and casted over and over again. That's Evrnu's goal for textile fibers. Our technologies enable them to stay in circulation, while maintaining their performance attributes."

The other significant development in their technology is sorting. Evrnu's sorting partner has created a camera that can identify, grade, and sort fabric. "To simplify, imagine a big scanner at the airport, when you look through things and it shows them in different colors. We optimized that system specifically for the textile industry," Stanev explains. The technology scans using a range of emitters from infrared to ultraviolet light but "stopping short of x-rays;" they agitate the molecules and emit light at different wavelengths, similar to a radar. "Every molecule vibrates depending on its structure, so we are taking this reading and using artificial intelligence to determine immediately if it's pure cellulose, if it's a modified cellulose like lyocell, or polyester." Then, the fabrics get separated into different buckets. He says it can sort up to one hundred different materials within a 0.1-percent accuracy of the fiber signature, including decorative trim, the content of the label, and even the type of thread used – which is important, as the recycling process demands precision.

As with most textile recycling, the final barrier is scale. "The technology exists," Stanev says. "We are making these fibers. We are looking for partners to scale." They are on track to deploy this technology at scale by 2030, working with global supply chain partners including Adidas, Stella McCartney, and Levi Strauss. In 2016, Evrnu partnered with Levi Strauss to create a pair of Levi's 511 jeans using five discarded cotton t-shirts and a small amount of virgin cotton. The partnership was Evrnu's first collaboration and was touted as representing a future full of new possibilities.

The possibilities presented by generating new textiles from waste are a fundamental part of transforming fashion's impact on the environment. This is not simply because they represent a solution to the issue of textile waste sitting in landfills – an issue that will only intensify until current rates of consumption are curbed. It is also because conversations about recycling textiles reveal how the entire lifecycle of a product needs to be considered at the design phase – in the ateliers of Paris and the studios of London. A circular fashion industry needs the decisions made by designers, while they're creating collections of pants, skirts, coats, shirts, and dresses, to be made with holistic awareness. How will the design function throughout the garment's use phase? Is it constructed in a way that means it is repairable? Will the fabric breathe against the skin? Is it durable? How will its materials and construction impact its recyclability? Will it have value after it's been loved and worn, in case its first owner wants to sell it or pass it on?

These conversations push the industry forward, to a place of responsibility. It's a place that seems alarmingly foreign in the take-make-waste world of fast fashion and hyper consumption. It's a paradigm shift, away from marketing and production schedules that insist on driving desire for newness, for the next purchase. A shift toward designers taking responsibility for the beginning and end of each garment's life and hopefully arriving at a place of heightened creativity, driven by the idea that each new garment can be part of the solution. Each garment can be made from waste or from fibers healing landscapes and constructed so they are able to be made and remade again and again.

Conclusion

Sometime during 2020, in between lockdowns, my brother and I drove out to visit a small alpaca farmer in northeast Victoria. It wasn't long after the fire season that had raged on for months and devastated 18.6 million hectares of the Australian landscape. The farms and bush we drove through were untouched this time, but the fires had left a mark on the locals. Each person we spoke to had experienced fires over years of living near the bush, and they had tracked the trajectory of these ones closely, knowing how quickly they can change direction. The threat to their land and their lives was imminent.

I was in Australia during that fire season. Each year, I tried to come home from Paris for Christmas, and that December, I spent a few days in Sydney for work. Every morning, the sun dawned red and angry over the city, a reminder that just outside its borders, expanses of bush were engulfed in flames. When I swam at Bondi Beach, there was ash in the water. A thin, filmy layer of black stuck to me – tiny dots of charred trees marking my skin – as I stood on the sand, drying in the sun.

Weeks later, I was back in Paris preparing for fashion week, and the fires were the talking point of every conversation. Climate change and its risks had never felt more urgent – until rumors of a new virus began to circulate. The Chinese buyers weren't traveling for the market at the end of January and, by Paris Fashion Week at the end of February, there had already been a COVID outbreak in Milan. Stores were running out of hand sanitizer, and people were starting to wear masks while the world scrambled to understand the threat COVID-19 posed. Fashion's two biggest manufacturing hubs, Wuhan and Northern Italy, were home to early and severe outbreaks that caused the industry's supply chains to grind to a halt. The industry declared it a moment to change. But now, more than two years into the pandemic, it's clear nothing really has. Fashion weeks have returned with the frenzy of models and media; the traveling show of editors, buyers, and designers; the cycle of newness and heightened spectacle.

In early March 2020, as the borders began to slam shut, I escaped Paris and flew home to Australia. The night before my flight, President Macron announced the French borders would close at midday. My flight was at 8 o'clock that morning. The roads were busy on the dark car ride to the airport; Parisians were fleeing the city for their country houses. We had no idea then what the virus meant and for how long we would be in and out of lockdown.

In the midst of the confusion, at what we now know was the beginning of the pandemic, my brother and I found ourselves standing at the top of a hill on an alpaca farm. The farmer who owned the property had gone to get her morning coffee and left us to gaze at her rolling fields and citrus trees. We were staring at a paddock that held three camels; they loped their way up the hill toward us when she returned, insisting on pats, trying to drink from her mug of coffee. When we got in the car later, my brother and I confided to each other that we'd confused the camels for alpacas when we first saw them – I didn't think alpacas were so big. She also had a small mill. She walked us through the various steps of turning a fleece into yarn: scouring, carding, combing, and spinning.

She presented us with the yarns and scarves they sold, each one softer and finer than the one before. Some of the product was mixed with possum fur, some of it had been dyed hot pink, bright purple, yellow, and blue.

I was a long way from Paris.

It surprised me how much work went into this raw material. How many sheep it took to make the wool we took for granted in design rooms and ateliers. How many processes there were between fleece and yarn and jumper. The experience truly emphasized the significance of the connection between our clothes and the land.

Right now, the regenerative fashion movement is just being established. Small-scale producers like this alpaca farmer and the farmers in Rebecca Burgess's Fibershed in California are doing pioneering work, testing models, and experimenting with novel ways to grow and harvest fibers. In some places, with some fibers, the ability to scale is more advanced – like Bombyx's silk factories in the mountains of China. Sometimes, the local industry has been operating for centuries, like Libeco in Belgium, but needs tweaks to move forward and put the earth first. But, what's most exciting is that important work has been started by industry leaders who can make the connection between farmer and designer, between producer and market. With organizations like Kering, Patagonia, the Savory Institute, the Ellen MacArthur Foundation, and Fibershed dedicating resources to research, training farmers, and fundamentally changing supply chains, the movement is already underway. Its potential is untapped and, significantly, its persuasive power is immense because it is a solution that grounds us in beautiful clothes and reduced consumption.

It's clear there is no other way forward. The earth is crying out for a new paradigm. From extreme weather events like wildfires and floods to pandemics that shut entire cities, the whole world – the earth – is demanding change. Demanding that we return to a time when nature was part of how we understood and interacted with the world around us. When we slowed down to consider and appreciate the beauty of what it offers us. Before clothes were produced and disposed of at increasingly high quantities and dismally poor quality. Before our wardrobes contained garments made of plastic. Before we abandoned the connection between our bodies and the things we wear on them. Before we lost sight of the landscapes and skills that imbue our clothes with value.

We cannot continue on the path of over-production and over-consumption we've been on, for two reasons. First, the limits of the earth are within sight, and as we are faced with the grim consequences of a warming planet, of dying reefs, rising sea levels, and more intense and severe weather, we will figure out how to live on this planet without destroying it, because we have to. But regenerative agriculture and fashion promise us more than just the opportunity to survive. They promise – and have already delivered – the restoration of grassy woodlands, of running creeks, the return of native plants and animals, healthy soils that sequester carbon and grow more fiber and food of better quality.

The second reason is that we are all tired of owning too much and feeling unsatisfied with the options in our wardrobes. For too long, we've been living with things we have no connection to – buying dresses, pants, and jackets we aren't even sure we'll wear. We are on the precipice of a new era of less consumption and more respect for the products we buy because we are reconnecting with their origins and the work done by farmers to cultivate the land that grows them. The relationship between the land and our clothes, between our clothes and our bodies, is significant – not least because we are wearing these materials against our skin. The relationship between design and comfort, between quality and enjoyment, between beauty and care, will dictate how we move forward to a place where we are only wearing clothes that we love, that make us feel beautiful, that we reach for knowing they will carry us through the day, that we will care for, mend, and pass on with joy. Clothes made of regeneratively farmed or recycled natural fibers.

Right now, the challenge is predominantly one of scale, which will be resolved with a variety of transitions. Yields will improve as landscapes heal and more farms shift to regenerative agriculture. Advances in technology and infrastructure for recycled cellulose materials will help, as will a decrease in demand, as our understanding of how we consume clothes changes. Achieving these goals won't make the transition to a truly "sustainable" fashion industry simple – but it is far from impossible. Production can be powered by renewable energy; pollution and chemical use can be curbed; and even though the road to rebuilding local supply chains is long, it is one worth embarking on.

In many ways, these shifts are inevitable.

Driving home from the alpaca farm, the roads were black and slick with rain. Green hills gently sloped toward the sides of the car. As the soft blades of grass whizzed by the windows, along with blurs of white lambs and sheep, the sun broke through the clouds on the horizon and beams of light hit the road, turning puddles into mirrors on the path ahead.

Notes

Introduction

1. Textile Exchange, *Preferred Fiber and Materials Market Report 2020*, June 2020, 6, https://textileexchange.org/2020-preferred-fiber-and-materials -market-report-pfmr-released-2/.

Chapter 1. There Is No Such Thing as Sustainable Fashion

1. *The Sustainability EDIT 2020 Industry Report*, October 20, 2020, 22, https://edited.com/wp-content/uploads/2020/10/The-Sustainability -EDIT-2020-Report-1.pdf.

2. Global Fashion Agenda, Boston Consulting Group, and Sustainable Apparel Coalition, *Pulse of the Fashion Industry 2017* (Copenhagen: Global Fashion Agenda, 2017), 8, https://www.commonobjective.co /article/pulse-of-the-fashion-industry-2017.

3. Morten Lehmann, Gizem Arici, Sebastian Boger, Catharina Martinez-Pardo, Felix Krueger, Margret Schneider, Baptiste Carrière-Pradal, and Dana Schou, *Pulse of the Fashion Industry 2019 Update* (Copenhagen: Global Fashion Agenda, Boston Consulting Group and the Sustainable Apparel Coalition, 2019), 1, http://media-publications.bcg.com/france /Pulse-of-the-Fashion-Industry2019.pdf.

4. Nathalie Remy, Eveline Speelman, and Steven Swartz, "Style That's Sustainable: A New Fast-Fashion Formula," McKinsey Sustainability,

October 16, 2016, https://www.mckinsey.com/business-functions /sustainability/our-insights/style-thats-sustainable-a-new-fast-fashion -formula.

5. "Infographic: Data from the Denim Industry," Fashion United, September 26, 2016, https://fashionunited.uk/news/business/infographic-data -from-the-denim-industry/2016092621896.

6. PE International, *The Life Cycle Assessment (LCA) of Organic Cotton Fiber: A Global Average*, Textile Exchange, 2014, https://store.textileexchange .org/product/life-cycle-assessment-of-organic-cotton/.

7. Dana Thomas, "The High Price of Fast Fashion," *Wall Street Journal*, August 29, 2019, https://www.wsj.com/articles/the-high-price-of-fast -fashion-11567096637.

8. Alden Wicker, "That Organic Cotton T-Shirt Might Not Be as Organic As You Think," *New York Times*, February 13, 2022, https://www.nytimes .com/2022/02/13/world/asia/organic-cotton-fraud-india.html.

9. Ellen MacArthur Foundation, *A New Textiles Economy: Redesigning Fashion's Future*, January 2017, 37, https://ellenmacarthurfoundation.org/a -new-textiles-economy.

10. Ellen MacArthur Foundation, *New Textiles Economy*, 20.

11. McKinsey & Company and Global Fashion Agenda, *Fashion on Climate 2020*, 2020, 5, https://www.mckinsey.com/~/media/mckinsey/industries /retail/our%20insights/fashion%20on%20climate/fashion-on-climate -full-report.pdf.

12. Elizabeth Cline, *Overdressed: The Shockingly High Cost of Cheap Fashion* (New York: Penguin, 2012), 166.

13. Ellen MacArthur Foundation, *New Textiles Economy*, 39.

14. D. G. McCullough, "Deforestation for Fashion: Getting Unsustainable Fabrics Out of the Closet," *Guardian*, April 25, 2014, https://www.the guardian.com/sustainable-business/zara-h-m-fashion-sustainable-forests -logging-fabric.

15. Nancy Harris and Michael Wolosin, "Tropical Forests and Climate Change: The Latest Science," World Resources Institute, June 2018, 1, https://www.wri.org/research/ending-tropical-deforestation-tropical -forests-and-climate-change-latest-science.

16. Changing Markets Foundation, *Dirty Fashion: How Pollution in the*

Global Textiles Supply Chain Is Making Viscose Toxic, June 2017, 14, https://changingmarkets.org/portfolio/dirty-fashion/.

17. Rebecca Burgess, *Fibershed: Growing a Movement of Farmers, Fashion Activists, and Makers for a New Textile Economy* (White River Junction, VT: Chelsea Green, 2019), 19.

18. Burgess, *Fibershed*.

19. Melanie Rickey, "Marc Jacobs: A Fashion Force to Be Reckoned With," *The Independent*, May 26, 2008, https://www.independent.co.uk/life-style /fashion/features/marc-jacobs-a-fashion-force-to-be-reckoned-with -834246.html.

20. Marjorie Val Elven, "People Do Not Wear at Least 50% of Their Wardrobes, Says Study," Fashion United, August 16, 2016, https://fashion united.com/news/fashion/people-do-not-wear-at-least-50-percent-of-their -wardrobes-according-to-study/2018081622868.

21. Ellen MacArthur Foundation, *New Textiles Economy*, 19.

22. Orsola de Castro, *Loved Clothes Last: How the Joy of Rewearing and Repairing Your Clothes Can Be a Revolutionary Act* (London: Penguin, 2020), 6.

23. Kate Fletcher, "Durability, Fashion, Sustainability: The Processes and Practices of Use," *Fashion Practice* 4, no. 2 (2012): 224, https://doi.org/10 .2752/175693812X13403765252389.

24. Ingrid Sischy, "Some Clothes of One's Own," *New Yorker*, January 31, 1994.

25. De Castro, *Loved Clothes Last*, 58.

26. Claudia D'Arpizio, Federica Levato, Filippo Prete, and Joëlle de Montgolfier, "Eight Themes That Are Rewriting the Future of Luxury Goods," Bain & Company, February 5, 2020, https://www.bain.com/insights /eight-themes-that-are-rewriting-the-future-of-luxury-goods/.

27. "Burberry Burns Bags, Clothes and Perfume Worth Billions," BBC News, July 19, 2018, https://www.bbc.com/news/business-44885983.

28. Kate Fletcher, "Exploring Demand Reduction through Design, Durability and 'Usership' of Fashion Clothes," *Philosophical Transactions of the Royal Society A* 375, no. 2095 (May 2017): 5, https://doi.org/10.1098 /rsta.2016.0366.

29. Fletcher, "Exploring Demand Reduction," 10.

Chapter 2. Fashion that Doesn't Cost the Earth

1. Chris Arsenault and Thomas Reuters Foundation, "Only 60 Years of Farming Left If Soil Degradation Continues," Reuters, December 6, 2014, https://www.scientificamerican.com/article/only-60-years-of-farming-left-if-soil-degradation-continues/.

2. Charles Massy, "Transforming Landscapes," *Griffith Review* 63 (February 2019).

3. Robin Wall Kimmerer, *Braiding Sweetgrass: Indigenous Wisdom, Scientific Knowledge and the Teachings of Plants* (New York: Penguin, 2013), 17.

4. Rebecca L. Oxford and Jing Lin, *Transformative Eco-Education for Human and Planetary Survival* (Charlotte, NC: Information Age Publishing, 2012), 316.

5. Charles Massy, *Call of the Reed Warbler: A New Agriculture, A New Earth*, rev. ed. (St Lucia, Australia: University of Queensland Press, 2020), 65.

6. François Baudot, *A Century of Fashion* (London: Thames and Hudson, 1999).

7. *Woman's Day* (Australia), May 3, 1954.

8. *Woman's Day* (Australia), May 17, 1954, 3.

9. "Karl Lagerfeld: Doing Fashion Today Is Like Being a Race Car Driver," *Huffington Post*, November 5, 2010, https://www.huffpost.com/entry/karl-lagerfeld-doing-fash_n_494842.

10. Andrew Barker, "Streamlining Collections: Paul Smith Reveals Own Fashion Calendar Fix," *Business of Fashion*, February 8, 2016, https://www.businessoffashion.com/articles/retail/streamlining-collections-paul-smith-reveals-own-fashion-calendar-fix/.

11. Luisa Zargani, "Giorgio Armani Writes Open Letter to WWD," *Women's Wear Daily*, April 3, 2020, https://wwd.com/fashion-news/designer-luxury/giorgio-armani-writes-open-letter-wwd-1203553687/.

12. Vanessa Friedman, "Designers Revolt against the Shopping Cycle," *New York Times*, May 12, 2020, https://www.nytimes.com/2020/05/12/style/coronavirus-shopping-cycle.html.

13. Alice Cavanagh, "In the Mood for Love, Fashion Gets Sexy Again," *Financial Times*, February 12, 2021, https://www.ft.com/content/2acbd7f8-6717-41c8-91cf-d4e04fd3aa5e.

14. Lou Stoppard, "Quarantine Made Me Long for Painfully High Heels,"

New York Times, March 9, 2021, https://www.nytimes.com/2021/03/09
/style/high-heels-corsets-covid.html.

15. Bridget Foley, "Bridget Foley's Diary: Tom Ford Says Fashion Will Come
Back," *Women's Wear Daily*, May 29, 2020, https://wwd.com/fashion
-news/fashion-features/tom-ford-coronaviris-cfda-1203643374-12036
43374/.

16. Massy, *Call of the Reed Warbler*, 20.

17. Food and Agriculture Organization of the United Nations, *State of
Knowledge of Soil Biodiversity: Status, Challenges and Potentialities* (Rome:
Food and Agriculture Organization of the United Nations, 2020).

18. Textile Exchange, *Regenerative Agriculture Landscape Analysis*, 2022,
https://textileexchange.org/regenerative-agriculture-landscape-analysis/.

19. Rachel Carson, *Silent Spring* (New York: Penguin, 2020), 22.

20. Massy, *Call of the Reed Warbler*, 165.

21. Gabe Brown, *Dirt to Soil: One Family's Journey into Regenerative Agriculture* (White River Junction, VT: Chelsea Green, 2018).

22. Massy, *Call of the Reed Warbler*, 235.

23. Kimmerer, *Braiding Sweetgrass*, 9.

Chapter 3. A Shirt Made of Flowers

1. Mile Socha, "Rei Kawakubo: Exclusive Q&A," *Women's Wear Daily*,
November 19, 2012, https://wwd.com/fashion-news/fashion-features
/rei-kawakubo-qa-6486260/.

2. Sven Beckert, *The Empire of Cotton: A Global History* (New York: Vintage,
2015), 97.

3. Keith Slater, *Environmental Impact of Textiles: Production, Processes and
Protection* (Cambridge: Elsevier, 2003), 128–97.

4. Rebecca Burgess, *Fibershed: Growing a Movement of Farmers, Fashion
Activists, and Makers for a New Textile Economy* (White River Junction,
VT: Chelsea Green, 2019), 133.

5. Chad Heeter (filmmaker), "Seeds of Suicide," *Frontline/World*, PBS, 2005.

6. Agricultural Biotechnology Council of Australia, *GM Cotton in Australia:
Celebrating 20 Years*, 2016, 4, https://www.abca.com.au/wp-content
/uploads/2016/12/Resource-Guide_Cotton_20years_2016_FINAL.pdf.

7. Gabe Brown, *Dirt to Soil: One Family's Journey into Regenerative Agriculture* (White River Junction, VT: Chelsea Green, 2018), 136.

8. "Dr. David Johnson's Research on Fungal-Dominated Compost and Carbon Sequestration," California State University Chico, accessed 10 January 2022, https://www.csuchico.edu/regenerativeagriculture/bio reactor/david-johnson.shtml.

9. Brown, *Dirt to Soil*, 136.

10. Changing Markets Foundation, *License to Greenwash: How Certification Schemes and Voluntary Initiatives are Fuelling Fossil Fashion*, March 2022, 55, http://changingmarkets.org/wp-content/uploads/2022/03/LI CENCE-TO-GREENWASH-FULL-REPORT.pdf.

11. Alexandra Freitas, Guoping Zhang, and Ruth Matthews, *Water Footprint Assessment of Polyester and Viscose and Comparison to Cotton* (The Hague: Water Footprint Network, 2017), https://waterfootprint.org/media /downloads/WFA_Polyester_and__Viscose_2017.pdf.

Chapter 4. La Dolce Vita and the Australian Merino

1. Gholamreza Sanjari, Hossein Ghadiri, Cyril A. A. Ciesiolka, and Bofu Yu, "Comparing the Effects of Continuous and Time-Controlled Grazing Systems on Soil Characteristics in Southeast Queensland," *Australian Journal of Soil Research* 46, no. 4 (2008): 348–58, https://doi.org/10.107 1/SR07220.

2. Christine Judith Nichols, "'Dreamtime' and 'The Dreaming': An Introduction," The Conversation, January 23, 2014, https://theconversation .com/dreamtime-and-the-dreaming-an-introduction-20833.

3. Bill Gammage, *The Biggest Estate on Earth: How Aborigines Made Australia* (Crows Nest, Australia: Allen & Unwin, 2011), 123.

4. Charles Massy, *Call of the Reed Warbler: A New Agriculture a New Earth*, rev. ed. (St Lucia: University of Queensland Press, 2020), 48.

5. Bruce Pascoe, *Dark Emu: Aboriginal Australia and the Birth of Agriculture* (Broome, Australia: Magabala Books, 2018), 13.

6. Bruce Pascoe, "The Imperial Mind," *Griffith Review* 60, May 1, 2018.

7. Marcia DeLonge, "Greenhouse Gas Costs and Benefits from Land-Based Textile Production," Fibershed, 2016, https://fibershed.org/wp-content /uploads/2016/10/LCA-wool-garment.pdf.

8. Rebecca Burgess, *Fibershed: Growing a Movement of Farmers, Fashion*

Activists, and Makers for a New Textile Economy (White River Junction, VT: Chelsea Green, 2019), 197.

Chapter 5. Cut on the Bias

1. Colin McDowell, "Madeleine Vionnet 1876–1975," *Business of Fashion*, August 23, 2015, https://www.businessoffashion.com/articles/news -analysis/madeleine-vionnet-1876-1975/.

2. "Vionnet, Couturier, Dies at 98; Innovator Created Bias Cut," *New York Times*, March 5, 1975.

3. Textile Exchange, *Preferred Fiber and Materials Market Report 2021*, 2021, 53, https://textileexchange.org/wp-content/uploads/2021/08/Textile -Exchange_Preferred-Fiber-and-Materials-Market-Report_2021.pdf.

4. Alden Wicker, "Why Does Silk Have Such a Bad Environmental Rap?" *EcoCult*, March 4, 2020, https://ecocult.com/why-does-silk-have-such -a-bad-environmental-rap.

5. "Silk," Responsible Sourcing Tool, 2022, https://www.responsiblesourc ingtool.org/commodities/69.pdf.

6. Max G. Levy, "The Race to Put Spider Silk in Nearly Everything," *Wired*, June 28, 2021, https://www.wired.com/story/the-race-to-put-silk-in -nearly-everything.

7. Rebecca Burgess, *Fibershed: Growing a Movement of Farmers, Fashion Activists, and Makers for a New Textile Economy* (White River Junction, VT: Chelsea Green, 2019), 110.

8. Global Industry Analysts, *Silk: Global Market Trajectory and Analytics* (San Jose, CA: Global Industry Analysts, 2021), https://www.researchandmar kets.com/reports/5030739/silk-global-market-trajectory-and-analytics; Textile Exchange, *Preferred Fiber and Materials Market Report 2021*, 9.

9. Textile Exchange, *Preferred Fiber and Materials Market Report 2021*, 53.

10. Livelihoods, "When a Tiny Silkworm Contributes to Bring Rural Communities out of Poverty: Livelihoods Launches a New Agroforestry and Silk Tree Plantation Project in India," Livelihoods Funds, July 7, 2020, https://livelihoods.eu/silk-bringing-rural-communities-out-of-poverty/.

11. Richard Kurin, "The Silk Road: Connecting People and Cultures," Smithsonian, 2002, https://festival.si.edu/2002/the-silk-road/the-silk-road -connecting-peoples-and-cultures/smithsonian.

12. Laura Bradley, "Alber Elbaz on the Fashion Calendar," *AnOther Magazine*,

September 5, 2011, https://www.anothermag.com/art-photography/1335
/alber-elbaz-on-the-fashion-calendar.

13. Ariel Levy, "Ladies' Man," *New Yorker*, March 9, 2009, https://www
.newyorker.com/magazine/2009/03/16/ladies-man.

14. Kate Fletcher, "Exploring Demand Reduction through Design, Durability
and 'Usership' of Fashion Clothes," *Philosophical Transactions of the Royal
Society A* 375, no. 2095 (May 2017), https://doi.org/10.1098/rsta.2016
.0366.

Chapter 6. Resort Wear from the Edge of the North Sea

1. Textile Exchange, *Preferred Fiber and Materials Market Report 2021*, 2021,
26, https://textileexchange.org/wp-content/uploads/2021/08/Textile
-Exchange_Preferred-Fiber-and-Materials-Market-Report_2021.pdf.

2. Claude Fauque, *Believe in Linen* (Tielt, Belgium: Lannoo Printers, 2008),
20.

3. Fauque, *Believe in Linen*, 20.

4. Danny E. Akin, "Linen Most Useful: Perspectives on Structure, Chemistry, and Enzymes for Retting Flax," *International Scholarly Research Notices*
2013 (December 2012), https://doi.org/10.5402/2013/186534.

5. Amy Lavoie, "Oldest-Known Fibers to Be Used by Humans Discovered,"
Harvard Gazette, September 10, 2009, https://news.harvard.edu/gazette
/story/2009/09/oldest-known-fibers-discovered.

6. Akin, "Linen Most Useful."

7. Textile Exchange, *Preferred Fiber and Materials Market Report 2021*, 26.

8. Fauque, *Believe in Linen*, 25.

Chapter 7. A Cashmere Coat Is the First Refuge

1. "About Cashmere," Sustainable Fibre Alliance, sustainablefibre.org/about
-cashmere/.

2. Textile Exchange, *Preferred Fiber and Materials Market Report 2021*, 2021,
47, https://textileexchange.org/wp-content/uploads/2021/08/Textile
-Exchange_Preferred-Fiber-and-Materials-Market-Report_2021.pdf.

3. Christina Archer, *Sustainable Cashmere from Mongolia: A Market Assessment* (Ulaanbaatar: United Nations Development Programme Mongolia,
2019), 9, https://www.mn.undp.org/content/dam/mongolia/Publications

/Sustainable%20Cashmere%20from%20Mongolia%20-%20A%20
Market%20Assessment.pdf.

4. Kate Abnett, "Solving the Cashmere Crisis," *Business of Fashion*, November 26, 2016, https://www.businessoffashion.com/articles/sustainability/solving-the-cashmere-crisis/.

5. "Responsible Cashmere Round Table," Textile Exchange Sustainability Conference, Vancouver, BC, October 15, 2019, 82, https://textileexchange.org/wp-content/uploads/2019/11/ResponsibleCashmereRoundTable-Vancouver2019.pdf.

6. Archer, *Sustainable Cashmere from Mongolia*, 6.

7. Mongolian Sustainable Cashmere Platform, "The True Cost of Cashmere," United Nations Development Programme, December 21, 2020, http://sustainablecashmereplatform.com/the-true-cost-of-cashmere/.

8. Bulgamaa Densambuu, Sumjidmaa Sainnemekh, Brandon Bestelmeyer, and Budbaatar Ulambayar, *National Report on the Rangeland Health of Mongolia: Second Assessment* (Ulaanbaatar, Mongolia: Green Gold-Animal Health Project, Swiss Agency for Development and Cooperation and Mongolian National Federation of PUGs, 2018), 6, https://jornada.nmsu.edu/sites/jornada.nmsu.edu/files/nogoon_english.pdf.

9. Mariana Simoes, "How Sustainable Cashmere Is Reversing Land Degradation in Mongolia," United Nations Development Programme, June 15, 2021, https://www.undp.org/blog/how-sustainable-cashmere-reversing-land-degradation-mongolia.

10. Abnett, "Solving the Cashmere Crisis."

11. Esha Chhabra, "How to Put the Luxury Back into Cashmere," *Vogue Business*, March 4, 2021, https://www.voguebusiness.com/sustainability/how-to-put-the-luxury-back-into-cashmere.

12. Market Watch, "Cashmere Market Size 2022," press release, March 15, 2022.

13. Mongolian Sustainable Cashmere Platform, "Swiss Green Gold Project Has Restored 5 Million Hectares of Rangeland in 8 Years," United Nations Development Programme, September 25, 2020, http://sustainablecashmereplatform.com/swiss-green-gold-project-has-restored-5-million-hectares-of-rangeland-in-8-years/.

14. Charles Massy, *Call of the Reed Warbler: A New Agriculture a New Earth*, rev. ed. (St Lucia: University of Queensland Press, 2020), 92.

15. Allan Savory, *Holistic Management: A Commonsense Revolution to Restore Our Environment* (Washington, DC: Island Press, 2016), 6.

16. J. J. Martin, "Keeping Ahead in Fashion's Slow Lane," *New York Times*, June 28, 2005, https://www.nytimes.com/2005/06/28/style/keeping -ahead-in-fashions-slow-lane.html.

17. The method was created in collaboration with the Jilin Agricultural University in China, the Academy of Science of Inner Mongolia, the University of Camerino in Italy, and the ENEA (Italian National Agency for New Technologies, Energy, and Sustainable Economic Development).

Chapter 8. The Endangered Forest

1. Food and Agriculture Organization of the United Nations (FAO) and UN Environmental Programme (UNEP), *The State of the World's Forests 2020: Forests, Biodiversity and People* (Rome: Food and Agriculture Organization of the United Nations, May 2020), xvi, https://www.unep.org /resources/state-worlds-forests-forests-biodiversity-and-people.

2. FAO and UNEP, *State of the World's Forests 2020*.

3. Nancy Harris, David A. Gibbs, Alessandro Baccini, Richard A. Birdsey, Sytze de Bruin, Mary Farina, Lola Fatoyinbo et al., "Global Maps of Twenty-First Century Forest Carbon Fluxes," *Nature Climate Change* 11 (January 2021): 234–40.

4. FAO and UNEP, *State of the World's Forests 2020*, xvi.

5. Jared Diamond, "The Erosion of Civilization," *Los Angeles Times*, June 15, 2003, https://www.latimes.com/archives/la-xpm-2003-jun-15-op-dia mond15-story.html.

6. FAO and UNEP, *State of the World's Forests 2020*, xvi.

7. Rachel Ehrenberg, "Global Forest Survey Finds Trillions of Trees," *Nature*, September 2, 2015, https://doi.org/10.1038/nature.2015.18287.

8. This figure is hard to independently verify, but viscose maker Lenzing attests that it "very roughly matches with their estimates."

9. Canopy, *Survival: A Plan for Saving Forests and Climate: A Pulp Thriller* (Vancouver, BC: Canopy, 2020).

10. "Rayon Fibers Market Forecast 2022–2027," Industry Arc, accessed January 9, 2021, https://www.industryarc.com/Report/16221/rayon-fibers -market.html.

11. Textile Exchange, *Preferred Fiber and Materials Market Report 2020*, June 2020, 51, https://textileexchange.org/2020-preferred-fiber-and-mater ials-market-report-pfmr-released-2/.

12. Paul Blanc, *Fake Silk: The Lethal History of Viscose Rayon* (New Haven, CT: Yale University Press, 2016).

13. R. Newhook, M. E. Meek, and D. Caldbick, "Concise International Chemical Assessment Document 46: Carbon Disulfide," World Health Organization, 2002, https://apps.who.int/iris/handle/10665/42554.

14. Changing Markets Foundation, *Roadmap Towards Responsible Viscose and Modal Fibre Manufacturing*, February 2018, 2, https://changingmarkets .org/wp-content/uploads/2018/02/Roadmap_towards_responsible_vis cose_and_modal_fibre_manufacturing_2018.pdf.

15. José Graziano da Silva, Achim Steiner, and Erik Solheim, "Forests: A Natural Solution to Climate Change, Crucial for a Sustainable Future," United Nations Environment Programme, October 3, 2018, https:// www.unep.org/news-and-stories/story/forests-natural-solution-climate -change-crucial-sustainable-future.

16. Canopy, *Survival*.

Chapter 9. Patagonia and the Ingenuity of Hemp

1. Yvon Chouinard, *Let My People Go Surfing: The Education of a Reluctant Businessman* (New York: Penguin, 2016), 102.

2. Tara Valentine, Emmanuel Omondi, and Andrew Smith, "Industrial Hemp Trial: Year 3 Results," Rodale Institute, January 20, 2020, https://rodaleinstitute.org/science/articles/industrial-hemp-trial-year-3 -results/.

3. "Hemp," Encyclopedia Britannica, accessed September 21, 2021, https:// www.britannica.com/plant/hemp.

4. Gregorio Crini and Eric Lichtfouse, eds., *Sustainable Agriculture Reviews 42: Hemp Production and Applications* (Cham, Switzerland: Springer, 2020), 40.

5. Textile Exchange, *Preferred Fiber and Materi- als Market Report 2020*, 2020, 21, https://textileexchange. org/2020-preferred-fiber-and-materials-market-report-pfmr-released-2/.

6. Chase McGrath, *2019 Hemp Annual Report* (Beijing: United States

Department of Agriculture, February 24, 2020), 2, https://www.fas.usda
.gov/data/china-2019-hemp-annual-report.

7. Textile Exchange, *Preferred Fiber and Materials Market Report 2021*, 2021,
25, https://textileexchange.org/wp-content/uploads/2021/08/Textile
-Exchange_Preferred-Fiber-and-Materials-Market-Report_2021.pdf.

8. Textile Exchange, *Preferred Fiber and Materials Market Report 2021*, 21.

9. Rebecca Burgess, *Fibershed: Growing a Movement of Farmers, Fashion
Activists, and Makers for a New Textile Economy* (White River Junction,
VT: Chelsea Green, 2019), 164.

Chapter 10. True-blue Recycled Denim from the Isle of Wight

1. Maxine Bedat, *Unraveled: The Life and Death of a Garment* (New York:
Portfolio, 2021), 27.

2. Leslie Kaufman, "Levi Is Closing 11 Factories; 5,900 Jobs Cut," *New York
Times*, February 23, 1999.

3. Kaufman, "Levi Is Closing 11 Factories."

4. Bedat, *Unraveled*, 25.

5. P. Smith, "Value of the denim jeans market worldwide from 2020 to
2027," Statista, February 16, 2022, https://www.statista.com/statistics
/734419/global-denim-jeans-market-retail-sales-value/.

6. Bedat, *Unraveled*, 24–28.

7. Dana Thomas, *Fashionopolis: The Price of Fast Fashion and the Future of
Clothes* (New York: Penguin, 2020), 77.

8. Damian Carrington, "Microplastics Found in Human Blood for First
Time," *Guardian,* March 24, 2022, https://www.theguardian.com/envi-
ronment/2022/mar/24/microplastics-found-in-human-blood-for
-first-time.

9. Textile Exchange, *Material Change Insights Report 2020: The State of Fiber
and Materials Sourcing*, 2020, 45, https://textileexchange.org/wp-content
/uploads/2021/05/Material-Change-Insights-2020.pdf.

10. Ellen MacArthur Foundation, *A New Textiles Economy: Redesigning Fashion's Future*, January 2017, 20, https://ellenmacarthurfoundation
.org/a-new-textiles-economy.

11. Textile Exchange estimates 26 million tons of cotton were produced in
2020.

Acknowledgments

I was very lucky to have the following people around me while I wrote this book. To say I'm grateful for their friendship and encouragement is an understatement.

To John, who was my first (and best) reader.

To Mum, who always insisted we practice spelling and grammar.

To Claire, who somehow knew when to ship me wine.

To Justin for being an excellent and generous sub-editor.

To James, Harry, Lily, and Margrethe.

To Siân for believing I could do this.

To Paul for connecting me with Black Inc.

To James for many hours of career counseling.

To Chloe and Albee for many detailed conversations about art direction.

To Imogen for her early encouragement.

To Maria for long walks by the sea.

To Jason for indulging me.

To Caroline for driving.

To Jesus for his photography.

To Mon and Josh for the swims.

To Kit for the late nights.

To Bayly for all the other times.

Thank you all so much.

To everyone I interviewed or who reviewed chapters: Glenn Rogan, Meriel Chamberlin, Rebecca Burgess, Angel Chang, Charles Massy, Helen Crowley, Hilmond Hui, Raymond Libeert, Sandy Fisher, Durl Van Alstyne, Shannon Welsh, Megan Meiklejohn, Chris Kerston, Daniela Ibarra-Howell, Krishna Manda, Rodney Keenan, Amanda Carr, Doug Fine, Alexandra La Pierre, Laura Balmond, Christopher Stanev, Anna Heaton, Andrew Joy, Harriette Richards, Darshil Shak. And to anyone else who found their way into the pages of this book. Thank you.

To Julia Carlomagno for taking a chance on me and commissioning this book. To Denise O'Dea, Jo Rosenberg, Chris Feik and the rest of the team at Black Inc. To Emily Turner and the team at Island Press. To Rosie McGuinness for the beautiful cover. Thank you.

This book is dedicated to my Dad. He was writing about the environment when he died, so it felt fitting to have his dictionary and thesaurus beside me while I wrote about it too. I miss him every day, never more so than when I submitted my first draft and wished he had been able to read it and make (unsolicited) suggestions that would have irritated me because of how much they improved it.

About the Author

Lucianne Tonti has worked in fashion in Melbourne, Sydney, London, and Paris. In 2020, she launched the sustainable fashion site Prelude, profiled in *Vogue*. Lucianne holds a Bachelor of Communication, a Juris Doctorate, and a Postgraduate Diploma in Political Science. She is the fashion editor of *The Saturday Paper*, a regular contributor to *The Guardian*, and her writing appears in *Australian Vogue*.